Published by
Enete Enterprises

6504 N Omaha Ave
Oklahoma City, OK 73116 (USA)

1st publication of
Becoming an Expat 101

Enete, Shannon 2014

Becoming an Expat 101 / Shannon Enete

ISBN-13: 978-1-938216-12-1
ISBN-10: 1938216121

Printed in the United States of America
www.EneteEnterprises.com

OTHER BOOKS IN THE SERIES

Becoming an Expat: **Costa Rica**
Becoming an Expat: **Ecuador**
Becoming an Expat: **Thailand**
Becoming an Expat **COOKBOOK:** Costa Rica

UPCOMING EDITIONS

Winter 2014: Brazil and Mexico Editions
Becoming a Nomad

visit: www.Becominganexpat.com

• to see updates in-between editions
• to join our newsletters
• for additional resources
• to discover what we come up with next!

DEDICATION

*To my gorgeous and adventurous wife who's always up
for my next crazy idea*

TABLE OF CONTENTS

INTRODUCTION

So you're exploring an international life, I'm excited for you. Reshaping my life as an international resident has been one of the most challenging and rewarding choices I've made. I'll tell you though, it's not for everyone. I'm not here to persuade you to ditch your life in your home country but to equip you to reach your goals and make an informed decision. No one country fits all, so it's up to you to explore your options and decide whether a country is a good fit for you.

This book is comprised of my experiences, research, and a hundreds of collective years of experience from numerous expats living in countries across the globe.

There are a variety of places on this earth that are extremely affordable, full of freedoms, and home to countless natural attractions. On the flip side of those liberties can exist disorganization, latency, crime, and inefficiency. The side that you choose to focus on will directly relate to your happiness and overall experience. More than twenty-five percent of folks who move abroad, return home within 3 years.

You'll notice that I have include a lot of additional resources via links or other books to read. The links are often "bitly" links for two reasons. One, they shorten the links, making them easier to input (sometimes the links are three lines long). Two, I can see what links you are most interested in, thereby learning how to serve you better in upcoming editions.

Keep an eye out for updates on www.BecominganExpat.com and www.BecomingaNomad.com for videos, articles, online seminars, and helpful resources on our website and Facebook Pages: *Becoming an Expat* & *Becoming a Nomad*

THE BASICS

THE A-Z TO A NEW WAY OF LIVING

People have been travelers or roamers since the beginning of time. We have moved west for a new frontier when happiness and or resources don't satisfy. With the current economy, healthcare structure, and challenges North America sees combined with the advances in technology that facilitate ease of an international life, I see the next 20 years as humanity's next migratory phase.

Each person has a specialized set of needs, wants, and environmental variables when fine-tuned equal the location he/she has most potential to grow. It would take out a lot of the guesswork if we all came with instructional stickers like plants do: "10-12 hours of sun daily, rainwater no more than 5 days out of the month, temperature range 50-88 F (10-30 C), urban living (or tropical, mountainous, etc), and a moderate social setting required." Since we don't come so equipped we have to do the work to determine what our sticker would read if we had one, and make the changes in our life in order to reach our ideal environment.

Just because you are born to a country does not mean that is the country you're destined to stay. I've spoken to many people who say, "I wish I could live like that." When I ask why they don't they say, "I could never leave Kansas, this is where my family lives, or I have too much stuff, or I am stuck here because I have a kids and a family." Where you live today and tomorrow is because of a direct choice you've made. Not making a choice is also a choice in and of itself. If you're born and raised in the America's Midwest and you hate humidity or the snow, then move to a climate you can breath easy in. Why not?

With Skype, Face-time, and frequent flier miles family is always a call or plane ride away. If you've decided that you must be with your extended family weekly, in person, in order to feel "right" or in your ideal environment then you have set that priority. If your conversation with me is dripping with jealousy than I'd say you need to re-evaluate your priorities. Remember living your best life doesn't do your extended family any injustice. They get a relationship with the best you! Plus, if you have kids, you can make the phrase, *settling in life*, foreign while the rest of the world is second nature.

CONSIDERATIONS

There are countless amazing countries with rich cultures and delicious cuisine. One of the hardest things about moving abroad is deciding what are your must have, what are your highly desireables, and how to sort out which countries satisfy them.

On a piece of paper write a list of variables that are important to you, such as: climate, cost of living, healthcare, education, hiking or kayaking, social aspect, ability to get a job or start a business, hospitable culture, language preferences, American styled homes (including kitchens), reliable high-speed internet, distance by plane to your home country, public transit, hot water, political stability, immigration process, crime, religious tolerances, view and treatment of women, etc. Now rate each category with a scale 1-10, ten being the most important and 1 being the least.

Now make a list of countries to consider as potential matches. Common countries to consider include: Malaysia, Singapore, Thailand, Vietnam, Ecuador, Costa Rica, Mexico, Panama, Ireland, Italy, Spain, Greece, France, Argentina, Chile, Peru, and Uruguay. The categories that you valued at 6 or higher (on the 1-10 scale) are your highly desired. If a country satisfies this country well then give it 2 points. If a contending country satisfies a less important category (ranking 5 and less) then the country gets 1 point. Evaluate all countries against all categories (each category providing the country with 0-2 points).

After you've completed the exercise, keep the top 3 countries as strong possibilities and test out each option throughout the rest of the book.

I strongly recommend visiting these top three countries prior to a final decision. You can do no better than see for yourself. All of the research in the world amounts to facts and subjective impressions from people with a different

arrangement of values,
desires, and needs.

TRY BEFORE YOU PRY

HOW RENTING PRIOR TO BUYING IN YOUR DESIRED LOCATION CAN SAVE YOU BUCKET LOADS, AND RENTING VS. BUYING YOUR DREAM HOME

I was a 911 paramedic in my "last life." In the emergency medical field, the mantra "Try before you pry" was a common and important one. When we approached a residence or car at an accident, we always attempted to gain entry by turning the handle before we broke the door down. This practice resulted in less damage and an overall better experience. The same can be true for your experience launching as an expat, you should peak past the door before you commit. Spending a year trying on a country could save you tons of money and psychological damage.

Try it on

Each country you may visit can be intoxicating with numerous natural assets, prices that cause your mouth to drop, and a pace that resonates with something inside of you. Which is why, after a brief visit, many people find themselves snatching up property while wearing "tourist goggles." Buying a house or property abroad should *NEVER* be done on a whim.

First off, you might be tricked if you don't do your homework. Second, you are viewing the country as a tourist. You really should live in your desired region for at least six months, better yet a year, to learn if it's a good fit. While renting a property, evaluate the area as a local and see what it's like after the honeymoon phase is over. Things like how often the water and electricity go out can re-direct your opinion on life in any particular region. Then, and only then, can you make a fully informed decision.

All too often expats return home with less money in their pocket. It's a common problem, because most literature out there is tied to sales. You read about Ecuador, Panama, and Costa Rica through a real estate agent's eyes, or through someone who sells familiarisation tours.

Certainly, there are times when you perform all your due diligence and your selected country just isn't the right fit for you. Many more times, however, people make the romantic leap into a tropical paradise without researching what exactly it entails. I can guarantee you, *it won't be a tropical version of your hometown!*

I enthusiastically urge you to budget an exploratory trip to experience different regions, and try them out by renting a place in each contending town. That way, when you do decide which region is your slice of heaven, you can rest easy knowing you have explored the country and your city is not only great, but better than all of the other good options you explored.

If you think that trekking around the country is not worth the cost or time, think again. Consider the added stress and cost of selling the house you regretfully purchased. Think of the life in your home country you sold away only to crawl back to later. You might be stuck in a foreign world for years before you can sell.

If you have an opportunity to rent the property you are thinking of purchasing, then all the better! You can see if the house is well built, if the plumbing and electricity are problematic, and ascertain the cost of general upkeep. Meanwhile if another buyer enters the scene, you would be given the opportunity to offer a bid of your own if you felt so inclined. A true win-win!

RENT

There is no denying my bias towards renting. The benefits are numerous!

- Try out the area with little to no commitment.
- Little financial investment, usually only requiring a deposit and first month's rent.

- Peace of mind that if something breaks, and it always does, you are not the one footing the bill.
- If you don't like your residence, community, or family circumstances no longer permit you to stay, you are free to pick up and leave.
- If the property proves to be a lemon, you can leave.
- If you are sensitive to the energy of a place, you can try it on and decide if you thrive there.

If you opt to rent make sure and ask the following questions:

- What your rental rate includes (homeowner fee, water, electric, tv cable, gas)
- Ask for an inventory list. Don't assume that just because your condo doesn't have a coffee maker you will get one. You accept the unit as is. If you don't like something about the unit,

negotiate changes before you sign.

Other common myths:
- If you decide to spend money on your own accord to "improve" the condo, don't assume you will be reimbursed.
- If you break your rental lease for whatever reason (even a death in the family), *you lose your security deposit*.

BUY

Just because I am clearly pro-renting before buying does not mean buying is without benefit:

- Continuity
- You are free to create your customized oasis, the dream home you always wanted
- Potential path for immigration (see the *Immigration* section)
- You have potential rental income

- You don't throw away money on rent (something that doesn't contribute towards ownership)
- You can personalize the heck out of your house
- A chance to gain equity if the value rises, which if you're in it for the long haul, is very likely to happen
- Often, a lower monthly housing expense, that is fixed and could be paid off over time

BEFORE YOU ARRIVE

Moving is incredibly stressful. In order to minimize the stress, cost, and errors, organization is essential. While I don't mean to belittle large domestic moves, you will have new obstacles like customs, passports, visas, immigration paperwork, and language barriers! This will be your first big test in flexibility, the most critical attribute (in my opinion) in order to have a successful experience overseas.

Not to worry, hundreds of people have successfully moved abroad before you. We've gathered all of their tips, and learned from their mistakes to bring you the following pages. Keep an eye out for checklists throughout the section.

SQUARE UP DEBTS

Living abroad is infinitely more possible and manageable without debt. The heaviest anvils weighing you down are your credit card, car payment, mortgage, and school loan debts (if applicable).

Create a new budget and ditch as many "wants" as you can, leaving only your needs. If you have decided to embark on a life abroad then that is now your biggest *want,* so keep that in mind when you sacrifice small things like HBO or cable.

In addition to ditching cable, start brown-bagging again and watch the savings pile up.

How to Retire Happy [1] by Stan Hinden delves deeper into ways to convert debt into retirement savings.

SECURE DOCUMENTS

Make certain you have secured all the paperwork needed before your departure. This will save months of frustration and hundreds of dollars. Each country varies on required documents, so read the *Becoming an Expat* guide for your country of interest or visit the government's site, or hire a visa specialist prior to your move.

If your driver's license or passport are going to expire soon, renew them now so they arrive before you depart! If you have children, make certain their passports and visa documentation are in order before your departure.

FOUR-LEGGED FRIENDS

Shipping your pets abroad has become fairly

---

[1] http://bit.ly/retirehappy

simple. More and more people are traveling and moving with their pets. Make sure your country doesn't have breed restrictions, like Ecuador (no Pit Bull or Rottweiler mixes or pure breads through their doors).

Most Countries Require Something Similar to the Forms Below:

☐ Get a Health Certificate (USDA form 7001) from your vet, **issued within 10 days of travel** by a USDA or CFIA accredited vet (North Americans).

☐ Dogs: proof of vaccination against distemper (Carre), hepatitis, parovirus (DHLPP), leptospirosis, parainfluenza, parvovirus, and rabies

☐ Cats: feline viral rhinotrachetis, panleukopenia (FVRCP), calicivirus, and rabies

☐ All vaccines except rabies must be administered *within 30 days* of departure to EC

☐ Rabies vaccines must be given *more than 30 days* but less than *12 months* prior to traveling to EC. The three-year rabies vaccine is not recognized in EC

☐ Tick & Tapeworm test must be completed within 21 days prior to travel

Pet Logistics

Microchipping dogs and cats has become a regular practice and is highly recommended. A microchip is a surefire way to prove ownership and is required for some pet transporter companies.

Once you have gathered your paperwork and have chipped your pets, you can shop for the best transportation for them. Make sure you're well versed in your airline's pet transport policy before you purchase your tickets. Some airlines restrict weight limits for in-cabin pets. Other restrictions often include maximum and minimum outdoor temperatures, nonstop flight requirement, and / or breed restrictions.

A good starting point would be to review the pet policies of the airline. A few major airline Pet Policies can be found below.

PET POLICIES

United:
http://bit.ly/unitedpetpolicy

American:
http://bit.ly/americanpetpolicy

Delta:
http://bit.ly/deltapetpolicy

US Airways:
http://bit.ly/USairwayspetpolicy

LAN:
http://bit.ly/LANpetpolicy

TACA:
http://bit.ly/tacapetpolicy

There are a few different routes you can go to get your loved four-legger to your new

home. With many airlines, you can carry your smaller pets on board in a pet carrier for a fee. If your pet is a service dog the fee is waved, and the pet does not need a carrier.

I recognize that there is a current trend where people fraudulently poise their dogs as service dogs. While I am an avid dog lover, I worry this will take away rights from the disabled.

Make sure you read the airline's policy (the included links) and not a third party's site. There are numerous out-of-date sources of information in cyber-land. The last thing any pet owner wants is to show up for their flight and learn you can't bring your four-legged baby.

If your pet is not a service dog, nor do they fit under the seat in a carrier, then your options are restricted to shipping them as checked luggage or hiring a pet transporter.

Pet transportation companies are the second

best option to riding in the cabin with you. They utilize smaller planes are often temperature regulated. First-class pet transporters even include a vet tech or other caretaker to monitor your furry children, assuring their comfort.

Services like Pet Movers are pricey but will actually deliver your pet door to door! They also provide you with a moving counselor who will help facilitate the best schedule and route so your pet has the fewest connections possible. Moreover, they provide the kennels used during transit, the kenneling when necessary for customs, shots and paperwork as needed, and obtain international import permits! They're also a member of the IPATA and USDA pet handlers.http:// bit.ly/petmovers

Shop around and find the best pet transporter that fits your budget and requirements. There are many scammers in the transportation sector. I recommend visiting www.ipata.org to shop for your transporter. Only reputable pet transporters are awarded certification through the International Pet and Animal Transportation Association (IPATA). The website also includes information about insurance, vets, animal handlers and more!

MAIL SYSTEM

You need to reshape your mail to suit your international living.
☐Make sure you unsubscribe from magazines, catalogs, and other snail mail subscriptions.
☐Start a list of people and companies that you need to inform about your move. You'd be surprised how long the list grows over a few weeks.
☐Set up online billing and electronic statements for

your bank, credit cards,
student loans, etc.

☐ Sign up for an absentee
ballot if you are interested
in keeping up with your
rights in your home
country.

☐ If you have a family
member or friend that's
extremely supportive and
wants to lend a hand, ask
them to use their address as
your base address and have
them email you pictures of
your mail as it arrives. If
you've you're your job well,
this shouldn't be too many
pieces of mail. This is a
pretty big favor so I
recommend occasionally
shipping their favorite
sweets via Amazon to them
as a thank you!

☐ Or invest in a mail service
like US Global Mail that will
provide you with a US
address, scan pictures of
your mail, and allow you to
respond via a smart phone
app with options to trash or
ship your mail to you. Plans
start at just $10 per month
for individuals.

BANKING

Does your bank serve you
internationally? Your local
credit union or large chain
bank might have served you
well in your hometown, but
as an international bank does
it fall short? Evaluate your
bank with the following
criteria:

• Can you fax a wire request
to transfer money?
• Are there ATM fees and if
so, are they excessive?
• Are there currency
transaction fee?
• If you're receiving a
pension, Social Security, or
annuity, can the payments
be automatically deposited
to your current bank?
(www.ssa.gov/foreign/
index.html)
• Do they offer mobile
deposits? (the ability to
take a picture of both sides
of the check and deposit
the check without ever
sending it in)
• Are they FDIC insured?

• Is there a minimum balance requirement to avoid maintenance fees?

Most banks charge a foreign transaction fee (a percentage of your purchase) each time you swipe your debit or credit card in a currency other than that of your country of origin. For example, if your bank charges a 10% currency transaction fee (CTF) and you buy dinner for $35 USD, your currency transaction fee will be $3.50 USD! CTFs add up quickly, as do ATM fees.

I didn't think to change banks before I moved abroad. In just six months, I racked up $210.67 USD in fees just to access *my* money! I now proudly bank with Charles Schwab and pay zero fees (information to follow).

Many towns around the world are still cash driven. Some small towns don't even have a bank or ATM. That's the exception however, more often cities have at least one bank.

Check to see what your bank charges each time you access your money from an "out of network" ATM. It's almost always the rule that the bank whose ATM you are using will also apply a fee. You could be looking at anywhere between $5-10 USD plus your currency transaction fee just to use the ATM!

You might conclude that your bank won't serve you well as an international resource. I've banked with Bank of America, Washington Mutual, and most recently Wells Fargo. I was paying way too much to access my money internationally, so I did some research and found a bank that offers everything I was looking for: Charles Schwab's High Yield Investor's Checking Account. *(I do not receive any kickbacks from CS)*

Take a look at the benefits:
☑ Zero maintenance fees

- ☑ Zero minimum balance requirement
- ☑ ZERO CURRENCY TRANSACTION FEES
- ☑ Free brokerage account
- ☑ Mobile deposits
- ☑ Online banking
- ☑ UNLIMITED ATM FEE REIMBURSEMENTS- not only do they not charge ATM fees of their own, they take it one step further and reimburse you for the ATM fees other banks charge you to access your money around the world!

The only other time I've heard of ATM fee reimbursement is through small credit unions.

Wells Fargo has an account that allows you to withdraw money twice a month without a foreign currency transaction fee (usual ATM fees will still apply). The kicker is, however, you have to maintain at least $25,000 in the account to avoid a steep monthly account maintenance fee.

CREDIT CARDS

Just mentioning credit cards cause palms to sweat and increase the heart rate for the folks who've fallen behind in the brutal credit arena. While this section might now suit everyone, for those people who can stay disciplined and organized you can reap some seriously amazing benefits by choosing the right credit card.

I recommend having at least two credit cards for emergencies if for nothing else. If you already have your favorite credit cards, make sure they don't expire anytime soon.

It seems like every time I travel at least one of my cards gets turned off due to a fraud alert. Even when I diligently call the card company ahead and report my travel plans. Having your cards turned off can be detrimental, which is why I always have three cards. I maintain two credit cards and one debit card, and I *never* keep all three on my person. I prefer to keep one credit card at home or in the hotel safe, and the other on me. I only carry my ATM card when I need to use it, otherwise it's in the safe with the back up credit card. When I'm in transit, I keep my passport, credit card, and ATM card in my travel pouch (under my clothes), and the other credit card and a small stash of cash in my zipped pocket easily accessible.

Do your credit cards reward your cost of living spending? Do they serve you? I just booked my one-way flight to Thailand for $15 and 40,000 points with United Airlines because I signed up for their Business Mileage Plus Explorer Preferred Card and was given 40,000 for spending $3,000 in the first three months. Now that is serving my needs just fine!

I also won't tolerate currency transaction fees. There are plenty of amazing cards that do not charge them.

Since I travel internationally, I look for cards with rewards for airlines that go to the countries I plan to visit, i.e. American Airlines and United.

I currently use the *Chase Sapphire Preferred* card and the *Mileage Plus Explorer*. Both of these cards dump into the same frequent flier pool. The Sapphire card allows me to transfer my points 1:1 mile into United's Frequent Flier program. In order to score this slick heavy metal card you must have decent.

Another option is the AAdvantage card offered through Citi Bank in conjunction with American Airlines. I've never enjoyed working with Citi, but I will say it's incredibly easy to redeem your miles anytime on flights around the world. I've flown no fewer than seven times with this card. The longest flight was from Santiago, Chile to Kansas City, USA. I paid $80 in taxes and fuel surcharge and used 30,000 miles!

If you have to make a purchase, you might as well make it work for you. The reason I switched to United from American was because American required that either my origin or destination be in the United States. United doesn't have this requirement.

I will give it to American, however, because their change fees are almost half of United Airline's, and they are excellent for last second flying opportunities.

ALL OF YOUR CRAP

Our belongings can cause a great deal of stress if not dealt with correctly. The first three questions you must ask yourself are: What do I need to take with me? What, if any, select items do I want to ship? Would it make more sense to buy new furnishings or send my house-full in a container? Take a mental inventory of everything in

your house. Out of everything in your cupboards, closets, and drawers, how much of it do you actually use on a regular basis? Many people are "collectors" with big houses to fill. Just because you own it doesn't mean you need to ship it.

The hardest decision about moving your belongings is whether to sell or donate everything and start fresh, or rent a container and deal with the daunting task of satisfying customs requirements.

STARTING FRESH

A new life with new stuff. You won't have to wait for your belongings to arrive, or deal with the hassles of importing into a foreign country. Instead, you'll have an open-ended ticket to shop for cool new local furniture.

In essence, it's a major spring cleaning of your belongings. Plus, selling off your old stuff could provide a nice chunk of change to help with moving expenses.

If starting fresh is your route, allow a few weeks or months to sell or donate everything outside of what you pack in your suitcases. Conquer one room at a time, leaving the kitchen for last since you will be using kitchen items up until the move.

Consider items that may be difficult to find abroad. I'm a 6'0" tall woman which is unheard of in much of Latin America and Asia. Besides curious stares, it translates to difficulty finding clothes and shoes that fit. Keep that in mind while packing. Craigslist, eBay, and Facebook groups are great resources when slimming down your belongings.

If you're a gadget geek like myself, make sure you have your electronic system set before your departure. Many countries don't have the latest devices available for sale, or if they do the import fees drive up the cost dramatically. It's better to be prepared then gamble with this one.

Every situation is different. For me, it doesn't make any sense to ship a container. I've never been attached to "stuff," outside of my electronics! I've moved regularly every 6 months - 2 years for the last 15 years, so I haven't accumulated much. In fact, I've worked very hard to constantly let go of things, so I can pack all of my worldly possessions into one duffle bag and a school-sized backpack.

The only kitchen item I maintain is an all purpose chef's knife (I love to cook) and I rent apartments/houses that are fully furnished and equipped.

Your situation may be drastically different, including kids, a house full of furniture, antiques, books that you want to reference, and other items you value and wish to keep.

CONTAINER

If you have the perfect furniture set (bedroom / living room), you don't have to part with it. Nor would you need to figure out where to buy furnishings in a new country with a language barrier.

If you choose to move forward with a container, make sure to purchase insurance for the contents. Also, research your moving company. Ask expats for referrals.

Take time to make this decision, it's a big one. If you decide on using a container, make sure you're prepared to wait weeks and sometimes months for your belongings. The average timeframe is 4-8 weeks.

INTERNATIONAL MOVERS

Finding the right moving company is key for any major move. Your moving company can mean the difference from having all of your belongings seized to a seamless tax-free experience. I speak aggressively not to scare you but to share with you the level of seriousness customs enforce regarding imports.

To begin your research, you can use search aggregators like www.intlmovers.com and www.moverreviews.com. The first allows you to enter your origin and destination locations, and they find companies that service your new and old areas. This allows you to request numerous quotes at once. The second website collects hundreds of reviews for the most popular movers. Compare your quotes to the reviews, BBB,[2] and www.movingscam.com before making a decision.

Ask for references from customers that have shipped to the country you're considering moving to and call them. Question the references about any damage and how the company managed those issues. Ask, *"Were the shippers on time and could you track your shipment throughout the process?"*

These websites are great for generalized moves. Since importing to any country requires specialty knowledge of said country, make sure to do the research to assure your company is well versed and experienced in these rules and regs.

OCEAN STAR INTERNATIONAL, INC.

While this mover maintains an A rating with the BBB and has been mentioned in Mover Mag and USA Today as one of the best moderately priced movers in the States, I cannot conclude that they would be the best mover due to some hellish stories I have read from their customers.[3] The short of it was, the client was guaranteed a lowball rate, then after all of their worldly possessions were gathered and across the globe, Ocean Star doubled their fee and held the belongings ransom. "Come get your stuff or pay up" was how they treated their customers.

REINER OVERSEAS MOVERS

I have read good things about Reiner in regard to international shipping to Costa Rica, Ecuador, and various other countries. I contacted them for a ballpark

---

[2] Better Business Bureau http://www.bbb.org/

[3] Read the full experience: http://bit.ly/movescam

quote to ship to Ecuador and here was their response:

"Did a ball park, 20 ft. 5000# lbs and came up with $9000.00 approx. including normal packing/loading, trucking the container from Oklahoma City to Houston for loading, ocean to Ecuador, customs clearance, and delivery to doorSalinas, Ecuador, unloading and unpacking, and same day debris removal. Excludes the port fees, from $1400.00 to 1700.00 and insurance, based on 2.50% of the declared value.

When you are ready for a free survey, let me know. I move lots of folks there, moving one of their Consul from Chicago at the end of the month."

Cesar Castro
Rainier Overseas Movers [4]
Director International Marketing

Container Experiences

Deana dropped $11k to ship a 40 foot container weighing 10,000 pounds from South Dakota, USA to Cuenca, Ecuador. She shares, *"I had an inventory list that was so specific, it was pages long. I believe it made a huge difference. There were no problems on the inspection because every box had a list of exactly what was in it. The inspector dug into the box, picked*

something up and found it on the inventory."

Clare Nowland reported:

*"My husband and I shipped 1/2 container (20 ft) door-to-door from New Jersey to Cuenca in June, 2014. **All States** handled the US portion of the move, and **INSA** the shipping to Ecuador. We paid about $1400 in storage fees, as our things were stored in Guayaquil for 2 months while we awaited our visas. But many of our tools and electronics were stolen; and a lot of glassware, one TV and the vacuum were broken. Even the Rubbermaid storage tubs were cracked and split, like they had been flung from a truck or container into the storage unit. Insurance is not available for a shared container which is opened and loaded into temporary storage, so we lost another $1400 in personal property. The initial cost for our shipment was about $3700. With storage, the total was $5000 for the 1/2 container. Our significant losses, most likely occurred when the container was opened."*

DOCUMENTATION

The most important part of your shipping process is: "pack list, pack list, pack list." Every person interviewed (professional exporter or

---

[4] http://bit.ly/rainierEC

expat) stressed the importance of the pack list, and how it was the critical component of their move. It must be 100% accurate, ordered sequentially, thorough, and all boxes must be labeled correctly. Any discrepancy will delay your container. Each day your shipment is delayed could incur a hefty storage fee. You can see how spending extra time to make sure the lists are completely accurate before you send the container is time well spent!

AVOIDING SCAMMERS

The moving company:

☐Should not ask for cash deposits before moving your items,

☐Should have a physical address near your area, not a P.O. box,

☐Should be licensed and insured,

☐ Should be a member of BBB (US side), and American Moving and Storage Association (AMSA),

☐Should conduct an in-home evaluation for an accurate estimate, or require a detailed inventory list.,

☐Be wary of low-ball prices,

See the end of this chapter for a moving checklist

SELLING YOUR CAR

Deciding whether to buy a car abroad can be tricky. The first time I moved internationally, I thought I would foot it everywhere. I'm apparently not as bad-ass as I thought. Within one week, I was looking on Craigslist for used beaters for sale.

You can easily sell your car a variety of ways: through Craigslist, the Autotrader, a used car dealer, or my favorite option, through Carmax. I have sold two cars to Carmax and really appreciate their quick and honest service. It was particularly helpful when my car was not fully paid off, because they made the process so simple.

I walked in and asked for a quote for them to buy my car. After about 25 minutes, their technicians had finished a review of my car and I was handed a printed guaranteed offer. I compared it to Kelly Blue Book, Autotrader, and Craigslist equivalents.

Sure, I would miss out on a few hundred bucks but selling with Carmax was easy, convenient, and I could decide what day to give up my baby. So, I returned to Carmax the day before my flight, handed the sales team the guaranteed offer (good for one week) and asked to complete the sale. Twenty minutes later, I walked out the door with a check! *(I also really appreciate purchasing cars with them, but that doesn't apply here, just thought I would share.)*

I have also sold and bought with Craigslist and the Autotrader. But after using them all, I really prefer Carmax because I don't have to worry about the individual I'm going to meet (at my house or some public lot), and there isn't the awkward haggling process. That to me, in addition to the added convenience of keeping my car until just before I left, was worth the difference in price.

ELECTRONICS & TECHY TIPS

This section was designed to help you create your best electronic solution system, or said more simply what gadgets you should take.

One gadget I recommend for any avid traveler or for those living abroad in countries that use cement walls in their residential construction is a booster[5]. With cement barriers your wifi signal, on average, won't reach beyond two rooms. I plug the booster in at the top of the stairs which then catches the wifi signal from my combo cable modem/wifi router and boosts the signal to the rest of the upper level. Since I'm on the verge of being a tech geek (I'm not savvy enough for the full title), I wanted to have access to the internet in each room of the house.

If you are moving to an area serviced by a cable provider, it's a good idea to bring your own cable modem/wifi router.[6] This way you don't have to rent one from the cable company and can bring up-to-date hardware avoiding unnecessary slowing or glitches caused by older electronics. It can be tricky if DSL is still wildly used which requires a different type of modem, so make sure and check if there is cable service where you plan to land. This is not a must have device, but is nice to have if you have the space to spare.

If you enjoy reading print books and magazines, the bad news is it will be more difficult to get your hands on English

---

[5] A device that picks up the wireless signal and repeats it (increasing the strength) http://bit.ly/boosteral

[6] A good wifi/modem combo unit: http://bit.ly/modemwifi

materials if you move to a non-English speaking country. There might be a few book stores that cater to expats if you're in a big enough expat community but don't count on it. You'll certainly be without your local Barnes N' Nobles and easy Amazon delivery. Electronic Readers are the most convenient solution. Sure, you can't smell the book or see how far you are by gauging the remaining thickness. You can, however, shop in the Nook, Kindle, and iBook store in addition to your library's free ebook download venue from the hammock in your villa, instantly downloading your next reading pleasure.

I recently sold my Macbook Air, Macbook Pro, and iPad for a Surface Pro 3. While I have been a huge Apple fan for more than two decades the Surface Pro 3 is the first device that can do everything I need it to do. Now I have one charger, one device, and just over one pound to carry. That's maximum minimalism. I mention this mostly because I'm excited about it, it might not be what's best for you. I'm entertaining a lifestyle that is very much on the move.

OTHER ELECTRONICS:
- Laptop or Surface pro3
- iPad
- Up-to-date smartphone *(who knows when you will be able to buy a new one)*
- Mobile speakers[7]
- Apple Tv[8] or Chrome for Windows users.

---

[7] Here is a link to an excellent waterproof bluetooth speaker: http://bit.ly/h20speakers

[8] a device that connects to your TV's HDMI input and allows you to sign into your Netflix and Hulu accounts, rent off of iTunes, and access and Apple computer music and video library right on your HD TV. Here is a link: http://bit.ly/appletv03

- Waterproof case[9] for your phone (for those refreshing downpours on your beach walks).
- External hard drive[10] to back up all of the amazing photos you will take.
- *Power surge protector-* you can pick this up in EC but make sure you use it. Lightening strikes have literally blown up appliances here.
- *Thumb/Flash drive* to take documents from your computer to be printed at a *Copia* store.
- *Video* camera and waterproof camera[11] with extra batteries *(what good is a camera if the battery is dead?).*
- Nice pair of *headphones* with a mic for Skype.
- 140W adapter[12] for your car (plug in your computer, camera charger, heat pad, or other 120V items while you're on long road trips).

STREAMING MUSIC AND VIDEO

What to do, what to do... Movie nights can be great entertainers, especially if you're in a location close to the equator where the sun goes down around 6pm year-round.

If you are accustomed to Pandora, Hulu, Instant Movies on Amazon, or Crackle, I have good news and bad news for you. At the time of my writing, they do not have many international licenses. The good news is you can download a free program to "bounce" your IP address. In laymen terms, the

---

[9] The best waterproof case for iPhones is made by LifeProof: http://bit.ly/lfeprof

[10] An easy to use, speedy 1T back up drive is made by Lacie: http://bit.ly/lacie1T

[11] This video camera is best for rugged outdoor adventures: http://bit.ly/goproexpat

[12] This is the one I have: http://bit.ly/140Wadapter

program will play hide-and-seek with the numbers that report to the internet gods where the connection originates.

The program that I use is called Hotspot Shield.[13] There are numerous programs, but not all are free. You can listen to all the music you want. Another option for music streaming is Spotify which has less international restrictions.

Depending on your country, Netflix may work just fine with a slightly different directory of offerings than what you are accustomed to in the States. Since there isn't a DVD subscription available, they offer more instant-watch movies. While the catalog is larger, they take away some instant watches that are available in the United States. I'm guessing the variance relates to the show's copyright restrictions.

If you are a movie freak and would love to host movie night at your house or in your backyard consider getting a portable screen and projector. Since it's dark so early, it would be a great way to spend some quality time with your neighbors!

BEST APPS FOR EXPATS

Jump into the app store and be immediately lost, intimidated, and frustrated. How do you find quality apps that will suit you? The best apps I've discovered have been mostly by word of mouth. As an expat who is a former Apple employee and a total Mac geek, let me share with you my favorite apps specifically with the expat in mind.

---

[13] To review or download this free program go to: http://bit.ly/ipbouncer

Skype

Probably, the most used and most valuable app for expats. This is a must have app. So you have downloaded Skype on your computer. Once you have a smart phone or tablet, download the free app and sign in.

I highly recommend making two purchases on Skype: an unlimited calling subscription (premium plan $60 a year) and a personalized phone number (another $60 a year). I purchased the subscription that allows unlimited calling to landlines and cell phones in the United States. I paid around $3 a month. Rates constantly change with different promos, but typically Skype rewards you for paying for the entire year in advance. The other purchase was just as important. If you don't purchase a number then businesses, family, and friends can't call you. While you can call them anytime you want, they will see a different number each time and not know it's you. You can choose your area code when you purchase a number.

I take Skype with me everywhere I can get cell service on my iPhone app. That way, I can make a call to loved ones or for business back to the States. If anyone needs to reach me and I have Skype logged in on my phone, it will ring!

There are competing apps that offer similar phone service such as Vonage, magicJack, and TextPlus. Skype has been at it the longest, has a proven track record, and adds video conferencing and instant message features. The second most popular internet phone service is magicJack.

Viber

Another free talk and text app that is growing in popularity, but unlike Skype it doesn't require invitation to connect to others. It automatically incorporates your phone book. The biggest drawback is those who you wish to communicate with must also be on Viber.

WhatsApp

In case you have been under a rock for the last 5-7 years, texting is practically required to keep in touch with people. I'm certain you know people who refuse to answer their phone, but will quickly reply to a text. International text messages get pricey if you don't know about great apps like WhatsApp.

Build a free account and text away! The drawback is the person whom you wish to text needs to be a WhatsApp user. This, however, is an extremely common and well established app, so it shouldn't pose much of a problem. The app is also a great way to send pictures without getting charged fees!

An alternative app that doesn't require your text-ees to have the same app is TextPlus. With TextPlus, you can choose a phone number (including the area code), and that number will be your texting number. You can send and receive texts on said number for free!

Voxer

"Breaker Breaker, Foxtrotter's on the move." I loved walkie-talkies as a kid. This app allows you to talk to other people just like you are both on walkie-talkies, or Nextels, except you aren't restricted to a 200 foot range. You can walkie-talkie with someone in Africa if they have the app and a cellular signal.

If you hate text messaging, you'll love this. If the second you get behind the wheel you need to text everyone, talk into the phone instead, and they will get your walkie message.

The downside of this app is the same as WhatsApp. The other user must also have the app downloaded, but they don't have to be logged in to receive the message. The app will notify them a new message is waiting to be heard. In order to talk back and forth in real time, both parties need to have the app open.

Google Voice

Google Voice allows the user to port their phone number to Google Voice and then forward it to a second number. Currently, they do not allow forwarding to an international number, but you can forward it to your Skype number!

It gets a little confusing, but basically you can tell Google Voice, via the set up on its website, which contacts you want to call and which of your phone numbers to use (i.e. the Skype number you purchased) then Google Voice will use wifi to make the call.

Other benefits include: multiple number call forwarding, a wide variety of voicemail options (different voicemail messages depending on the number dialed), an excellent spam call filtering, and voicemail transcripts via your email!

You must set up Google Voice from the States. It will not allow you to do so once on ground in Ecuador. To learn more about how Skype and Google Voice can integrate see: http://bit.ly/skypegv

XE Currency

This app is exactly what it sounds like, a currency converter. While Ecuador uses the dollar, it's nice to have in case you decide to visit neighboring Peru or Colombia.

Google Translate

A translator app every expat should have in their arsenal is Google Translate. Even if you are not in the smart phone arena, make sure and take advantage of Google Translate on your computer. The biggest drawback of the app is that it requires cellular service or wifi to work. If you are struggling with the same word, however, it remember previous translation requests.

Word Lense

This app was recently acquired by Google. You open the app and click record on a sign you wish to translate. Word Lense instantly translates anything in print using your built-in video camera in real time!

TripIt

As an avid traveler, I love this app! It's the ultimate travel organization resource. Sometimes I book my airfare, hotels/hostels, and rental cars months out while other times only days ahead.

After I downloaded TripIt, created an account, and authorized it to access my email, I no longer needed to worry about printing or organizing my confirmation emails. I used to search my email for these confirmation codes, reservation codes, etc. Now, because TripIt recognizes when I receive an email confirmation, it automatically adds the information to the app!

TripIt also allows you to create trips. I recently returned from a three month trip to South America. I was able to separate all of my reservations by creating multiple trips, each one defined by a span of dates: Machu Picchu trip, Ecuador trip, Wedding Trip, and Honeymoon trip. It was so great to see all of my complex plans organized so clearly without an ounce of effort on my part.

After I set the dates, any new confirmations for those dates automatically got added to the corresponding trip. I was able to access my trip plans on my iPad, iPhone, or any computer by going to Tripit.com. How great is that?

TripAdvisor

This app is great if you are on the move. My wife and I take last-minute road trips frequently, and TripAdvisor really helps us find hotels, attractions, and outdoor activities. I love the "near me" option. It's a great *save me* app when I don't do my homework! The downside is it's super slow. The lag factor is really annoying, but if you use it in a restaurant or hotel with wifi, it's not *as* bad as on 3 or 4G.

Convert Units

This is really only needed if you are from the US. Since the United States is hell bent on being different, we don't know: what a price per kilo gets us, if we are speeding at 50 kph, how much space is $1000m^2$, or how large 2 hectares of land is. Until you learn these new measurements, an app like Convert Units is very helpful.

Kindle

Everyone has heard about the Kindle. What you might not have heard is how hard it is to find books written in English in Ecuador. Unless you are in Cuenca or other large expat community, it can be very difficult. So even though I prefer a book in my hand over a screen, I have completely sold out to the Kindle App. It's nice to have all my books in my skinny iPad and iPhone.

Kindle just added *Kindle Unlimited* which offers unlimited reading for one monthly fee of $9.99. Interestingly enough, it was launched just a few short months after two other companies offered monthly subscriptions for unlimited reading.

I chose the Kindle App as my primary reader over iBooks and the Nook because as an Amazon derivative, it is often $2 or $3 cheaper than the Barnes N' Noble's Nook. All three programs have similar interfaces, so no deciding factor there. The Kindle has more inventory than any other book app. Even though I am a Mac geek, I don't see any Apple oohs and awwws like I usually do regarding their reader. I miss Steve Jobs…

Overdrive

Use your library card and download free eBooks to *Overdrive* for your reading pleasure. Thousands of libraries use Overdrive, check to see if yours does. Why buy books when you can get them for free! If you don't have a library card, get one before you leave. All you need is a photo ID with a local address or an ID and a piece of mail with a local address. It's a no brainer! You will even have access to free magazines and newspapers.

Oyster

If you read so much that the library offerings won't cut it and you would prefer a book over watching a movie on Netflix, then you may want to consider a subscription with the book version of Netflix, Oyster. With one monthly rate of $9.95, you can read unlimited books anytime, anywhere! They have a free trial, so check them out if it sounds up your alley.

Dropbox / GoogleDrive/ OneDrive

Dropbox has been around the block many times now and is still the cloud service leader. There are numerous competitors these days: Onedrive, ShareFile, CX, Cloudme, TeamDrive, Egnyte, Huddle, Cubby, Syncplicity, Box, Amazon Cloud Drive, Wuala, SugarSync, and SpiderOak to name a few. I'm sure that many are just as good as Dropbox.

I am in the process of switching form Dropbox to Googledrive because I'm using Google everything, and Googledrive has a built in feature in my email and chrome browser offering me added ease of use. The rumor is that Onedrive will be launching unlimited storage for everyone, which may tempt me to jump clouds again, but I'm not holding my breath.

A free subscription caps at 15 GB which is plenty for thousands of documents. I have many of my documents and manuscripts backed up for my publishing business on Dropbox. You can pay $9.99 a month for 1000GB of cloud service with either GoogleDrive or Dropbox. I primarily use an external drive for my video production company, and a second external hard drive to back up my entire computer (including my pictures and video content).

Don't be caught without a backup in the States or abroad. You cannot recreate the memories captured in your thousands of pictures. I'm also sure you don't want to re-create that presentation for work or rebuild your music collection.

If you choose to land in the tropics, your computer liability increases. The humidity is like kryptonite to your hard drive, sand is the devil, and you can be sure that both will be in your computer if you live near the beach..

Flickr

With Flickr, everyone is given 1TB for storage of photos for free. That's roughly 500,000 photos (the figure varies greatly depending on your resolution). You can even set it up to automatically save photos that you are taking on your smart phone instantly! Flickr can be used as an excellent online backup resource so you don't lose those priceless experiences so meticulously captured on camera! Plus you can easily share albums with friends via email or Facebook. Speaking of Facebook...

Facebook

While you may not have been a "Facebooker" in the past, once you live in a different country you may re-think your stance. Facebook provides a way to stay connected and informed in your loved ones' lives. You can see pictures from their trips, watch their children grow up, and comment on each adorable photo, making a virtual appearance in their lives when a physical one isn't possible. You can also share your adventures in Ecuador.

I know from experience that people love seeing new exotic places. After seeing some of your gorgeous photos, they might be compelled to plan a trip to visit you!

Photocard

The post office system in Ecuador is flawed at best. Packages arriving empty is not uncommon. Postcards usually make it to the States but take 4-8 weeks! Photocard is a cool app that lets you assign a picture you have taken on your iPhone/ iPad as the postcard cover, then allows you to write a message in a variety of fonts and sizes. It even has stickers so you can decorate the card. Once completed, you purchase one credit for $2.99 to have it printed and put into the US mail that day! Two to three days later, your grandkids, buddies, parents, or clients will be surprised with a fun, personal, and customized card from you!

Weather Underground

I enjoy the interface of this weather app on the iPhone. One standout is it's hyper local specific reports. It utilizes social interaction to assure the accuracy from one neighborhood to the next. Other pluses: it's incredibly user friendly, gorgeous displays for forecasts, wind speed, precipitation, sunrise/sunset data, and has an easy to use radar feature. You can also easily add different cities around the world to the app so you can call up your family and ask them how the snow storm is coming along.

Google Maps / WAZE

Both of these apps are great GPS resources. I personally have utilized Google Maps as my primary routing app. There was only one instance living in Costa Rica where Google Maps didn't have the roads I needed to reach my destination (in this instance, Rio Celeste). Surprisingly enough, Mapquest did have the roads in question. My adventures in Ecuador were 100% satisfied by Google Maps.

WAZE is a fun to use GPS app that also has social data such as eyewitness accident information, police checkpoints, and more. It allows you as the user to add up-to-date information about an accident you passed, a broken down vehicle, or a cop with a radar gun locked and loaded! So if you're stuck in traffic, open up WAZE and see what the holdup is, or better yet, check WAZE before you commit to a route.

Juice Defender Plus

Run this app to extend battery life on Andriod-operated smart phones. I could say something snide like, "Apple doesn't need an app like this because of their superiority," but now that would be rude!

For those of you who scoff at how technology can help you enjoy an international life with the remarks, "I moved here to get away from all of that." This section was clearly not for you. To each their own, right?

SET UP YOUR COMMUNICATION SYSTEM

UNLOCK YOUR PHONE

Almost all phones purchased in North America are locked by their original carrier so only sim cards provided by the carrier will function with the phone. Make certain you can unlock the phone for use in Ecuador. Otherwise, the phone is no good to you as an expat.

First determine if you are under contract with your service provider. If you are, you must either finish your term or pay a steep early cancellation fee. After your contract has expired or terminated and you have a zero balance on your account including your phone, you are legally entitled to an unlocked phone.

Each carrier handles the unlock differently. AT&T has a customer service department that is "suppose to" unlock your phone after receiving a written request and the phone's IMEI number. I tried this route numerous times for my iPhone with no response. I found that using $10 and a third party service was the way to go. There are numerous services that do an excellent job providing you with a factory unlock (i.e. no hacking) within 24 hours. One that I have used successfully numerous times is:
http://bit.ly/unlckphone

T-Mobile's policy is if there is no balance remaining on the purchase of your phone, they will unlock it. Simply dial 611 which directs you to their customer service. Tell them you are going on a trip abroad and need the phone unlocked. It may take them up to 48 hours to complete the unlock.

If you have a phone with Verizon, Sprint, MetroPCS, Cricket, or U.S. Celluar, then it's time to go shopping because they are CDMA phones and will not work in most of Ecuador. CNT has a very small network for CDMA service, but it's basically a joke. I believe it's best to just leave it behind in the States.

Ecuador is in conjunction with the rest of the world on the GSM network. If this is all Greek to you, pretend that GSM is on one radio station and CDMA is on another but the dial is broken. The US decided to be different (shocker right?) opting for the CDMA network when it

was new and exciting. So you can put your old phone next to your yardstick on your way out of the country.

BANDWIDTH

Make sure your phone supports the bandwidth that the country you're considering uses. You can go to www.phonearena.com and enter in your phone to find out which frequencies it supports.

SKYPE

Features:
- ☑ Skype to Skype calling
- ☑ International calls
- ☑ Call waiting
- ☑ Video
- ☑ Messaging
- ☑ Sharing
- ☑ Personalized number
- ☑ Smart phone app

If you are not already a Skype user then go to www.skype.com and create a new account. Take care to remember your user name so you can give it to your loved ones. After you create an account, make sure all of the people that you wish to "Skype" have also created accounts. Make a few trial runs to work out the bumps. Call up your mom, daughter, son, or BFF and ask them to login. Stay on the phone in case they encounter "technical difficulty." Test video conferencing, instant messaging, voice calls, and sending pictures or files over Skype. That way, when you're thousands of miles away, you will know how it works and the process required.

If you choose Skype as your main source of international communication, you will want to purchase a personalized phone number and subscription. See the *Communication* section in *After You Have Arrived* for more information.

TEXT MESSAGING

Texting has become a form of communication to keep in touch with our younger generation. In fact, there is a whole new language being created around texting. BRB... Ok, I'm back!

International texting gets pricey fast! There's a solution with a few excellent apps that allow you to text for free. *I use WhatsApp and TextPlus which I spoke about in **Best Apps For Expats***. Your Skype account will allow you to text but it will cost you. The amount is displayed in the lower right corner of the texting space. It usually ranges from 9-15 cents per message. You must add "Skype credit" before you can text.

magicJack

☑ International calls
☑ Call waiting
☑ Transfer your number

☑ Use a regular phone!
☑ Smart Phone app
☑ Caller ID

The most popular internet phone services are Skype and magicJack, hands down. If you prefer to use a wireless phone or even a wired phone at home, magicJack has some extraordinary gizmos so you don't have to take the call through your computer. Skype has come out with a few gadgets [14] recently to respond to the magicJack Plus.

MJ also has free call waiting! You are required to purchase the device that translates the cable-modem signal to a phone jack receiver. You will need a regular phone or computer to use the magicJack. You can either transfer your number or select a new one. They provide a 30 day free trial, but you are required to pay a subscription. If you decide to go with the magicJack, make sure and order the device before departure and bring a phone with you so you can take advantage of all the options.

DATA

Some people experience difficulty setting up their data services with their iPhone, iPad, or other smart device using international service providers.

APN settings are settings in your phone that occasionally need to be adjusted in order to assure your data plan functions correctly.

Once you have a sim card and are able to make calls, turn off the wifi and check to see if you can receive your email or search the web. If you can, then you don't need to make any adjustments to your APN settings. If you can't, then this is most likely the hurdle keeping you from

---

[14] See some of the options ranging from $20-$100: http://bit.ly/skypephne

connectivity. If you have no idea where the setting is located, Google "Where is the APN setting on a ____ phone?"

Moving Checklist

☐Go to www.intlmovers.com and get quotes and companies that serve your two points of location

☐Ask for recommendations from friends, expat forums, AREC, and read testimonials found in this chapter

☐Double check with the BBB regarding the potential company

☐Find out what the mover will do if an item is damaged in transit

☐Obtain at least three estimates from various companies and compare their costs with their corresponding services and ratings

☐Find out if the mover is registered with FMCSA. http://ai.fmcsa.dot.gov/hhg/Search.asp?ads=a

☐Determine when and how your items will be picked up

☐Acquire all contact information for the movers for each step of the process: before, during, and after the move

☐Purchase insurance for your items

Moving Day

☐ If at all possible, be present to answer questions and oversee work

☐Watch the inventory process and make sure the condition of your items is correctly documented because this list is used to calculate your taxes

☐Keep your bill until you have all possessions in your new home and all claims are settled if applicable

☐After the truck drives away, perform a final walk through so you don't forget anything

☐Make sure the appropriate party has directions to your new home!

☐If your contact info changes, update it with the movers and drivers

Delivery Day

☐Be present to answer any questions, inventory the boxes, and direct traffic

☐Supervise unloading and unpacking (if applicable) of your goods

☐Make sure the inventory list reflects any damaged items before you sign any documents

☐Pay your driver or sign documents authorizing payment according to the terms of your agreement

After You Arrive

You have arrived after you step off the plane, through the jetway, and out the doors where the warm moist air greets you (in the tropics), or the cool dry wind zips across your face in the mountains.

Welcome to your new life as an expat. Make sure to soak up this moment, celebrate it! Don't rush past it, you are no longer in a hurry. Settle into the rhythm of the country you've chosen as your new home.

If you were unable to make an exploratory trip to check out each region and secure housing, make sure to plan for at least a few weeks of exploration, and hotel/hostel expenses while you find your rental. The last thing you want to do is jump into the first rental you see, since the region and your home will greatly affect your overall satisfaction with life in Ecuador. The more places you tour, the better suited your selected home will be.

FINDING A RENTAL

North Americans and Europeans are planners. We

want to know exactly where we're going, how long we will be there, and exactly how much "there" will cost. This way of living doesn't completely jive with each country in the world. Much of the world is on a much more relaxed pace with less connectivity to the internet. While it is possible to arrange your accommodations ahead of time and sign a lease for a year before you land, I highly discourage it. If you don't wish to spend the beginning of your trip looking at houses and regions then I suggest you take a separate "scouting" trip sometime before the actual move.

If you're hoping to land along the coast, be aware that the rental market is very fluid. Ecuadorians and gringos often visit for shorter spans of time which causes a large flux in inventory. In mountain regions like Cuenca, people are usually looking long term. Since the coast is seasonal, the prices double in the high season and triple during the holidays. For a high season rental (Christmas through Easter), try to make arrangements by August or September.

A scouting trip dedicated to hunting for rentals and exploring potential cities is a necessity! This is the best time to discover how close or far the grocery store is, and where the bus station or gas stations are. After you have viewed at least 8-10 homes, write down a list of must haves and wants to see which home suits you best. Assess the regions by using the W-A-S-P acronym discussed in the *Where is Your Haven* section.

PURCHASING A HOME

If you haven't yet, read the *Try Before You Pry* section before you proceed.

The first step is to gather referrals for an excellent

attorney or broker making sure the referrals are from people who actually purchased property through him/her. Then set up an appointment and ask any and all questions you have about purchasing property after you have read this guide.

Next, start searching for properties in your desired location. If you opt to have an agent assist you, look into what regulations are in place for real estate agents in your country. There may be zero regulation which equates to people running around calling themselves an agent, but have zero knowledge about the laws and market.

Ask what their commission is upfront and get it in writing. That way if it ever changes for any circumstances, you have it in black and white.

Many countries don't have exclusive agent agreements, so feel free to shop around and see which agent you like the best, and who shows you properties that are closer to your wish list and budget.

PURCHASING A PROPERTY

If you have constructed a home in the United States then you are familiar with the seemingly endless details that are required in order to make a quality home. Add to that, minimal regulation, a language barrier, and a confusing permit process and you have a true international adventure! On the plus side, labor might be cheaper than you're accustomed to, depending on what country you choose.

Oftentimes, there are numerous lots for sale. Peruse at a slow pace. Consider potential growth, access to public utilities, and infrastructure. Remember, many of the owners of those lots you are drooling over are selling them because they made a hasty purchase. Do your research, and live in the area where you are considering buying prior to purchasing. Purchasing a lot is a fairly quick process, selling one can take years.

When house or property hunting, take into account you are in a new culture. Business is conducted differently than in your home town. Take time and ask around to discover the best business practices.

Lesson two, let's say you successfully secured a meeting with the owner. If you pull up in a fancy car, dressed to the nines, displaying fancy jewelry, you will have likely tanked any chance at a low ball offer. Much of Latin America and the Caribbean citizens already think you, as a gringo, are rich. Now they are certain you are rich and the sky is the limit with their selling price.

INTERNATIONAL BANK LOANS

Most expats who arrive with the intention of buying, arrive with cold hard cash in order to secure their new abode. For those of us who have "eggless-nests" options are slowly creeping our direction. If you buy directly from a new construction agent in an ongoing construction project, the construction company can often provide you with a financing option.

There are also people who have secured personal loans from their banks located in their country of origin. It can be a long-shot, but if you have a good history and relationship with a smaller bank, sometimes they will go to bat for you.

OWNER-FINANCING

This is not a popular route, just yet. It's a bit of a long-shot. However, we are seeing a slow increase in owners willing to jump into this potential mess in order to secure a buyer.

There are a variety of different arrangements with owner-financing so make sure you are comfortable with your terms. Be careful to choose a structure that protects both the buyer and seller.

SQUATTERS

The last thing that any homeowner wants is a squatter in their house. In the United States, it's a health, safety, and financial hazard. In Ecuador, Costa Rica, and other countries that have squatter rights you're in danger of losing your property. *Listen up part-time expats!* Squatters can have rights to your diggs!

If squatters occupy your "unoccupied" house and land and work for a period of time, they can accrue property rights. Eventually, they can apply for its expropriation from the "absentee landlord." There have been instances in rural towns on foreign-owned land where a large organized group of squatters entered the land and created make-shift shelters. Due to their size, it was much harder to evict them.

What do you do if you find out a squatter is on your property? You must immediately file for an eviction order. If you catch it early and you can prove that, the procedure could be simple. However, the powers that be tend to favor the squatters.

When purchasing a house, take extra care to make sure signs of squatters are not present. If there is a caretaker of the property, make sure they really are a caretaker and not a squatter that may already have rights to the same property you seek to purchase. If you are concerned about squatters, film your property frequently so you have proof of improvements and changes demonstrating the property is not abandoned.

If you plan to leave for an extended period, make sure you have a caretaker on the property to keep squatters out. You can place an ad in the "Caretaker Gazette" or other house sitting sites (listed in the **How to Live for Free** section) for someone to house or pet sit your property. You provide the chores to be completed daily and the time span they will reside on your property.

In exchange for taking care of your property, they receive a free place to live! It's a win win! Create a written contract that each party signs so that he/she cannot become a squatter. In addition, have a neighbor or close friend that you trust keep an eye on the property, popping in to say hi, and check out the place every few months.

LOCAL BANKING

To open a local account or not to open a local account, *that* is the question... There are pros and cons to establishing a local banking solution. Most expats opt to utilize a local bank for monthly bills such as cell phone, cable, groceries (ATM card), and rent. All things considered, opening an account opens doors for you.

Pros

- *Access to services-* You'll need a local account for many services. Some cell phone and internet providers require a bank account.
- *Replacement-*If you lose your bank card, it's easier to get replaced because it's in country.
- *Risk control-* Using your local card is also better for managing risk because you will never have large sums of money in said account.
- *Bill Pay-* You have many more bill pay options with

local banks, which means less errands and less lines to wait in.

- *Street credit*- Drop that local card, yes, you are a local!

Cons

- *Hassle* - Initial hassles setting up the account
- *Risk*- Whatever money you have in the account is not FDIC insured and might not be as secure.

John, an expat from Toronto, Canada who also works in Ecuador, shares his opinion about local banking:

"My Canadian income stays in Canada and my Ecuadorian income gets used here. Taxes are paid to both countries but only on the income earned in each country.
Service charges are the issue as the Canadian banks charge $5.00 per transaction (at least that is what mine charges). Using ATM's is the best way to get cash. Since my pension is deposited into a Canadian bank that I have access to through ATMs, I don't need to have a bank here.

The only reason to open an account here would be to use the bank as a method of paying bills.

I opened an account at the same bank that my employer uses (I am an expat but I am working here for a few months.) in hopes it would make the process of cashing or depositing my cheque easier. It helps a little. I still need to show my passport to cash the cheque and access my money. The account is available through local ATM's but the daily limit is ridiculously low. Sending money back home is VERY expensive (5% of the amount being transferred, if it is over $1000.00, or $55 if less than $1000.00)."

Getting it Done

Most countries and banks require the following paperwork:

- Application (filled out during your meeting)
- Passport in hand
- Residence Card
- Proof of address
- Letter of recommendation (From someone who has an account at the bank you are applying at. They must sign it with their account number and residence card or passport number.)

- Minimum deposit
- Copies of
  everything.

LOCAL COMMUNICATION

CELL PHONE

If you have a CDMA phone (Verizon, Sprint, UScell, or Cricket), it's no good in most of the world. It's best if you purchase a GSM phone[15]. Don't forget to insure that it is unlocked and not under contract with a provider! *See more about unlocking your phone in the* **Before You Leave** *section.*

Take your passport, your unlocked GSM phone, and about $10 USD to a local wireless provider. Ask around to find out which provider has the best coverage. Purchase a new prepaid sim card, and put the rest of the money on the account so you have some minutes available for use. It's not as easy to keep your number on prepaid phones as it is in North America so if you change companies, you often can't port your number.

If your town doesn't have internet providers, or you wish to have internet on the go with your laptop or other electronic device, you can purchase a 3G stick or hotspot device with the local cellular providers.

INTERNATIONAL COMMUNICATION

Hopefully you've already set up your Skype account (or other provider mentioned), subscribed to the best unlimited calling plan for your situation, and purchased a unique phone number where business connections and loved ones can reach you. If not, read *Communication Set Up* in the **Before You Arrive** *section.*

---

[15] GSM phones in laymen's terms are the phones that use sim cards

If you have a smart phone, launch Skype and make a test call in the app. Make sure to dial from the Skype app, otherwise you will use airtime and long distance fees will apply!

Confirm that everyone you want to contact has a Skype account and knows how to log in. For the technologically challenged, I highly recommend you assist them in setting up their Skype so you can test out the connection.

To add someone to your Skype contacts, click "Contacts" at the top of your screen, then "Add Contact," then key in either their Skype username if you have it, or the email that they used to set up the account. This procedure needs to occur on both sides before you can be seen online and available for chatting on Skype.

Download and install TextPlus on your smart phone as mentioned in the *Before You Arrive* section. Send a trial text message to a loved one and have them send one back. You are up and running!

Don't forget about FaceTime for those who have Apple products. You can either connect by using their cell phone number or their Apple ID email address. Each route is free utilizing wifi for the connection.

TRANSPORTATION

Your transportation solution can make or break your budget. If your worried about your monthly overhead one of the best things you can do for yourself is move to a place that is pedestrian and public transit friendly. Another cheap solution to this chronic problem is picking up a used scooter to manage day to day errands. They are cheap and gas efficient. Depending on the country you land in the cost for purchasing a car could be double what it is in your home country due to high import tariffs.

In addition to the purchase of the vehicle you will have insurance, registration (safety inspection), maintenance, repairs, and fuel expenses to look forward to.

GATHER YOUR BEARINGS

The most frustrating part about moving for me was I had no idea where to get anything. For example, I needed an extension chord, an aux cable, and an adapter to go from the old stereo in my condo to an aux cable input. I hadn't the faintest clue where to find any of these items. I also had no idea how to say "Aux cable" in Spanish. My best shot was "hay un cable que usa para eschucar música en el carro?" Which is a really poor gringo way to say, "is there a cable that you use for listening to music in the car?" See what I mean? Stuff that usually requires zero brain power suddenly gobbles up endless energy!

In San Diego, I would simply Google Map the nearest Target and be on my way. Not so much in other countries that aren't as "connected" as the US. Even if there was an obvious retail outlet for my wanted item, there isn't an online venue to search the location of the nearest store. Many stores don't register with Google, so they don't show up in a search. This is why your landlord, expat community, and local friends are priceless resources. They've already hunted down many of the items that you will need and want. If they haven't looked for it themselves, their buddy has and found it. Your network is gold! They will help answer:

☑ Where is the grocery store?
☑ Where is the gas station?

- [x] Where is a good mechanic? (referral)
- [x] Where can you buy hardware items?
- [x] Where can you buy furniture?
- [x] How do I find a handyman?
- [x] Where do I pay my water bill?
- [x] Where can I recharge my cell phone?
- [x] When in doubt, roll with the flow, wait and then wait some more.

ESTATE PLANNING

Having your affairs in order is important no matter where you live. When you add the extra complication of an international residency, you need to take extra care in your arrangements for the unfortunate possibility of personal or spousal demise. Death is scary, horrible, and unavoidable... So we need to plan for it. We don't want to leave our grieving loved ones in a bind. That's the last thing anyone wants.

Consult an attorney from your home country to see how to organize your will to assure that your international residency won't complicate matters. If you purchase property, cars, or maintain bank accounts abroad you should create a will for those international assets with an estate planning attorney in your international location.

Some countries have laws regarding your estate, take Ecuador for example. In Ecuadorian law your children are the first heirs to the estate, after which follows parents, and if there aren't living children or parents then it falls on living siblings. If your will does not agree with this order it will be null and void managing Ecuadorian assets. Look into the country you choose and see what is required, if anything, for your will.

Take care to include your burial or cremation wishes in the document. This decision is extremely personal, and in some circumstances religious. I will warn you, repatriating a body to your home country will cost you a fortune (if it's not covered with your insurance). Plus, it can be a bit logistically challenging if the body is leaving the hot and humid coastal region.

CHECK LIST

☐Make a budget to kill your debts.

☐Assess your current bank and credit cards for international compatibility. Make changes as applicable.

☐Obtain or renew passport(s).

☐Renew drivers license if applicable.

☐Gather immigration documents needed.

☐Decide what to do with your stuff.

☐If shipping a container, request at least three estimates from reputable movers.

☐Decide which electronics you want to take with you and purchase the electronics that you need for the move.

☐If you are a smart phone or tablet kinda' gal/guy, download and play with the best apps for expats.

☐Make sure you have an unlocked GSM phone.

☐Create a Skype account and share it with loved ones and business colleagues.

☐Download a free text messaging app and try it out. Give your contacts your new texting number before you leave.

☐Prep your car for sale, advertise and sell *(Carmax is a great option I have used twice)*.

PART IV

FAMILY & EDUCATION

MOVING ABROAD WITH KIDS. DOES IT HINDER OR HARM THEIR FUTURE?

MOVING WITH A FAMILY

Uprooting your family in the pursuit of something better is a scary prospect. North Americans have been conditioned from a very young age that their homeland is the best and most sought after country in the world. The truth is, the best is not the same from one family to another. One country does not fit all.

I'm compelled to remind you there is nothing new about seeking social and economic opportunities elsewhere. Humans are migratory beings. Long before the westward movement, people migrated to richer pastures in order to increase their quality of life and, in some cases, to survive. I am a strong proponent of thriving not surviving.

With big business encroaching on middle America, education at a record low, healthcare costs seeming endless, poverty and unemployment at record highs, and quality of life on the decline, many people have decided now is the time to look elsewhere.

Below are a few important questions commonly asked by parents considering migration:

Would I be helping or hindering my children's growth and opportunities? Would we be able to return if we decided it was best for the kids? Is it safe? What is the cost of school?

Moving your family from your place of residence is an extremely personal decision. My goal is to fully inform and answer any questions you have so you can make the best decision for your family. Remember, no decision is a decision in itself. Now, let's address these common concerns.

EDUCATION ABROAD

The most important criteria for many expat parents is accreditation. They want their children to have as many options and open doors as possible.

There are often a few degree options that a child can earn while attending school abroad:

☐ The local highschool diploma which makes your child eligible to apply for college in-country.

☐ The International Baccalaureate (IB) Diploma, accredited by the International Baccalaureate Organization in Geneva Switzerland is the most flexible option. This degree makes you eligible to apply for college in the USA, Europe, and Latin America.

☐ The USA High School Diploma is available at every American private school and online through the many homeschool programs (i.e. K-12). This diploma enables you to apply to colleges in the USA, Europe, and many other countries.

Expats have the same three options for schooling that their peers have in their hometown: homeschool, private school, and public school (except for places like Thailand where one of the parents must be Thai in order to enroll their child in public school).

Oftentimes, foreigners choose to place their children in private English taught schools so their child acclimates more smoothly, without a language barrier. Others opt for full immersion through placement in schools who speak the local language so their children will become bi-lingual more quickly. The latter option is harder for the first six months to a year but after the hump, their kids are bi-lingual and thereby can acclimate easier with their newly acquired language skills.

Now for the *good* news! There are a variety of ways to homeschool and obtain a US or IB diploma for little to no money! Also, there are hundreds of private English-taught schools across the globe.

HOMESCHOOLING

Homeschooling has gained popularity both in the States and abroad. The only difference is really where "home" is. Homeschooling abroad can be challenging when considering activities designed for groups of participants of the same age.

K-12.com

This site allows you to navigate through international education options from a variety of schools ranging from public to preparatory. If you maintain an address in the US and pay taxes in that state (*maybe a family member's address for your mail)*, you can select the corresponding state and enroll in online public school.

Many states require you to start the program while in-state, so make sure to set up your education options before you leave the area. In-person "Start-Up Success" sessions are often provided to introduce the student to the online learning setting. While you're there, they also develop customized Individualized Learning Plans (ILP). If your program requires textbooks, make sure and get as many as you can prior to leaving. Purchasing books and shipping them to EC can be a bit of a hassle (see *Mail* in the *Before You Leave* section).

Most K-12 programs offer college level courses so that your student can begin to earn college credits while in high school!

Go to www.k-12.com to learn more.

PUBLIC SCHOOLS

Would I be helping or hindering my children's growth and opportunities?

Don't take my word for it. Schedule an appointment with potential colleges and employers in respectable fields. Ask them how they would respond to a potential student or employee with international experience. What I believe you will discover is that an international upbringing adds quality, diversity, and growth that no other program or school could match.

At the very least, your child will be bi-lingual, have successfully acclimated into another culture and way of life (huge points in both college entry and employment), and have learned life skills and experienced self-growth unmatched by a peer that remained in the United

States. I would have loved an international upbringing.

Outside of resumés and college entry brownie points, your child will learn about nature through experiencing it with all five senses! There is no museum required in order to experience biology in Ecuador, Cost Rica, Thailand, Panama, and other countries in the tropics. Gone are the days the football team acquired the monies previously allocated for the arts.

Home life could refocus around the family. An affordable family centric life is the norm and the expected way of life in much of the world. Since life is less expensive, you would be able to take breaks from your work to play with, talk to, and shape your own children's lives! Gone are the days of depending on daycare or school to raise YOUR children, a dream come true for many!

Your path would not be without bumps. The transition time may be very difficult on you and your kids. If your kids are adolescents, it can be particularly rough. Language acquisition will be harder and their self-consciousness will hinder their language expression. Teenagers undoubtedly experience hardship finding their place in the world. They want to be different and the same all at once. If you add a new culture and language into an already volatile time, you can expect an explosion.

That being said, every child is unique and how they handle change can be dramatically different from child to child. Moving abroad could be the best thing you could do for your teenager. Only you know what's best for your kids. Don't let society or me tell you what your kids need.

Would we be able to return if we decided that it was best for the kids?

The answer to this question is very much dependent on your planning. If you're not fully committed to the idea of moving your family abroad, why not commit to a year? Save up enough emergency cash to fly everyone home and pay for at least three months of bills.

If you own your home and have gained a handsome amount of equity, you have a choice to make. You can either cash out, have your safety pile of cash, and rent in Ecuador, or you can hire a rental agency to rent your US home and rent in Ecuador.

The risk is not equal for each option. If you choose the cash out option and Ecuador doesn't work out, then you could possibly have a difficult time finding a comparable house or the same interest rate you locked into years ago.

The market, however, is unpredictable. Take the market in 2002, for example.

If you had sold and moved away from California just before the crash, you would have likely doubled your money! Decide what's most important to you, the money upfront or the security of owning a home with potential rental income.

As far as schooling goes, if you were homeschooling, your kids won't miss a beat. If your kids were in an Ecuadorian school, there may be a bit of re-acclimation but no unsurpassable hurdles there.

Work

As far as work is concerned, why not take your work with you? You would be surprised how many jobs are telecommuting friendly.[16] If your employer or your industry is not, start looking for something else that is, or start something new!

If you packed your work and took it with you then

---

[16] See the Telecommuting section for more information

you would not be at risk of losing your income by moving abroad or globe trotting for that matter. In fact, the move would have increased your marketability. You could add: bi-lingual, an international specialist, or an international consultant on your brag list.

Is it safe?

Safety is on every parent's mind. I don't mean to be too philosophical but what is safety? Do rules make it safe? Do low criminal statistics make it safe? Safety to me is a feeling, a vibe. I have felt very safe in countries with lax on the rules and dependency on the police.

Many countries that your peers would think unsafe really pale in comparison to the US, the land of a mass school murders, terrorist attacks, gangs, and other violent crimes.

I don't believe the statistics accurately represent each population because many cultures don't report incidents, instead they take matters into their own hands.

In most countries around the world, children are free to roam the streets and play with the neighborhood kids without fear. While the cities are not crime free, the international norm is not fear-driven as it is in the States. To live life more freely, what a gift that could be to your child!

ACCLIMATING THE CHILDREN

ADJUSTING TO A NEW SCHOOL, LANGUAGE, ACTIVITIES, AND EXPLORATION

If at all possible, plan your move so the kids have time to acclimate before school starts. Hire a private language tutor for them and you while you're still living in your home country. Make language acquisition a family endeavor. Play language Jeopardy, Apples to Apples (in the new language), or other language games together for game night

After arriving to your new country, sign up for intensive language classes as a family for at least two weeks, preferably a month. You might not all be in the same class because your language levels may vary, but you will all be able to practice your speakign together which will greatly assist your adjustment. If you or your spouse is struggling with the move, it will certainly reflect on your children's experience. So set yourself up for success.

ACTIVITIES

Make sure that moving abroad is an adventure for the kids. You may have visited your country in the past and the kids enjoyed it as a vacation. This expectation is hard to come back from when transiting vacation life to real life. Make sure and plan fun activities.

Let them be part of the planning process. Give them assignments like "Explore the back yard and see if there would be a good spot for compost or a small garden." If they're old enough, have them research how to compost and build a compost bin / drum / stack for use in your yard. Find ways to connect their hobbies with the natural assets Ecuador has to offer. My teenage brother-in-law built a zip-line and platform 50 feet up a tree with his dad! Other activities could include:

☐Creating a scavenger hunt consisting of flora and fauna, birds, and frogs known to be in the area for them to take a picture of and identify. Then compare notes and see how many points they got! Reward the points with a trip to the beach, park, pool, or nearby waterfall!

☐Bring a picnic to a nearby waterfall and enjoy the serenity.

☐Feed the iguanas.

☐Go on "adventure walks" together with a wildlife guidebook, learning and identifying new plants, insects, and animals each day.

☐Take Spanish lessons from the same school and have homework sessions together.

☐Once a month, let a child pick somewhere new to explore within a given range. If you can afford a weekend away once a month or once every two months, this would be a great way to get to know the country.

☐ Google "solar carving" and learn this fantastic way to use the sun's energy as your paint brush by engraving the wood through burning! A much better use of the magnifying glass than killing ants! Pick up a cheap pair of welding glasses from a hardware store.

☐ Buy cheap digital cameras (possibly disposable) and have photo contests! The winner gets to choose what's for dinner from a list of possibilities!

☐ Put a blanket down on the ground outside after dark and star gaze. Use an iPhone app, Skywalker, to help you identify the constellations. You can either tell the corresponding Greek mythology stories or make up new ones. You start the story then tag the person to your right to continue the story, and so on.

Key points to keep in mind are: language acquisition, change of schedule and expectations, making new friends, and getting them connected in the community so they have a sense of purpose. For teenagers, it is of utmost importance that they make it on their own. Support any healthy hobbies or interests they express. Make sure they have the freedom to find things that interest them.

When you run out of ideas, Pinterest is an excellent resource. Just search for things to do outside, craft ideas, gardening, things to do for free, and so on!

PART V

WORK & BUSINESS

A GUIDE TO STARTING A BUSINESS ABROAD OR OPERATING ONE
INTERNATIONALLY

WORK HARD PLAY HARD

Not Retired?

You're never too young to move to EC. It's a land for the wise, the adventurers, and the peace seekers. Herds of 20 and 30 somethings dissatisfied with the rat race are looking for alternative lifestyles elsewhere.

Without the hurdles of large industry that encompass entrepreneurship in the US, an international startup is exceedingly more possible these days. Start up fees are modest, and if your new life abroad is significantly cheaper you have more wiggle room in the first formative years of your business.

Whether your new business is registered in the US, EC, or South Africa, you must satisfy a need in order for it to be successful.

Examine your market and see where gaps exist. If you hope to serve the community you live in, find out what needs are not being met. If you hope to serve an international community online, find a niche that you are passionate about and can easily satisfy from any location in the world.

Once you decide what type of business you want to create, set out with a business and marketing plan.

One side of my business, Enete Enterprises, entails filming and producing two minute marketing videos for adventure tours, destinations, hotels, real estate, and special events. In various countries in the tropics, I can stroll into a hotel or tour agency with my iPad and easily obtain an audience with the decision maker and share what I can do for them.

In the US, it takes months of redirection, red tape, and dismissals before I may or may not gain an audience with the decision maker.

There is a huge market for tourism, niche group travel, retirement, medical tourism, eco-living, alternative living, health, and self-sustaining properties just to name a few.

Check out how your country performs in the World Bank Doing Business report for 2014,[17]

CREATING A BUSINESS ABROAD 101

Take time to consider the best way to incorporate and the location in which to file your business when you enter the world of entrepreneurship. Ask your experienced accountant about incorporating prior to

---

[17] For the full report: http://www.doingbusiness.org/data/exploreeconomies/ecuador

doing so. Incorporation requires a great deal of paperwork and expense and provides little to no benefits. Once incorporated, you are held accountable to countless ever changing laws and in order to dissolve the corporation, you will spend months completing the paperwork and nursing the resulting paper cuts. The take home message is really do your homework prior to taking action. Oftentimes it might be better to start out as a sole proprietor.

Consider your market. Are they locals, businesses, are they North Americans, or is your service or product without borders?

If after seeking counsel from experienced business owners, and speaking with a local attorney you have decided to start a business and register it abroad, you will have a variety of things to do in order to make the ball roll. Some to-dos may include:

- ☐ Reserve the company name

- ☐ Hire a lawyer to prepare the minutes of incorporation

- ☐ Deposit capital into a bank account set up under the name of the company.

- ☐ Have your lawyer present the documents above (with copies of the charter and the Bylaws) to the appropriate party for the approval of the company's incorporate.

- ☐ Publish an abstract of the charter in a daily newspaper that circulates where the company operates.

- ☐ Apply for a tax ID.

- ☐ Receive inspection and operations permit from the municipality.

Some countries require a minimum capitol pay in.

Also, look into the laws for foreign owned businesses.

DOING BUSINESS

In order to be successful, you need to learn about your new home's work culture and how to incorporate it into how you do business.

North Americans are often quick firing, wheel and deal type of business people. If you're quick and to the point in the US, the time saved is greatly appreciated since time is the highest valued commodity. That business culture doesn't translate or get the job done in every country. Instead, regular social gatherings, sharing meals, and talking about your family might be what gets the job done elsewhere.

Some countries focus on trust. They can't trust what they don't know. Because of this you may be drilled over every aspect of your private and public life before a local commits to working a deal with you.

Time management might also be drastically different in your new country than your home town. In Latin America, your employees could arrive to meetings one to two hours late without apology (because it's the norm). Learning to account for this rule will save you many headaches.

HIRING / FIRING EMPLOYEES ABROAD

Before you decide to hire locals for your business or to clean your house, study the labor laws carefully. They might be drastically different from the laws in your home country.

Make sure and create a well worded contract if you decide to employ a worker full-time.

In some countries, order to fire an employee the employer, must obtain authorization from the Ministry of Labor and Human Resources. It's like a game of *Mother May I* but with much more paperwork. You can see why it's important to understand what you're getting into with a clear grasp of labor laws prior to hiring.

Many folks decide that for their small business it makes more sense to avoid all of the complications of hiring full-time staff by hiring independent contractors (IC). So instead of hiring two full-time workers, they might hire 4 ICs.

I hire ICs off of Elance and Odesk to complete various skills for me: eBook formatting, cover art, design, logos, etc.

TELECOMMUTING

An increasing number of companies are seeing the win-win in telecommuting. They can lower overhead with utilities and real estate costs, and increase employee morale and productivity by allowing them to choose the environment they thrive in.

If your employer doesn't currently use telecommuters, don't worry, it doesn't mean they won't allow it. You must be savvy and take care how you present the offer. I recommend you read The Work From Home Handbook[18] by Diana Fitzpatrick and Stephen Fishman before you pitch to your boss. The book will help polish your pitch in order to speak their language and address their fears or concerns, before they even realized they had any.

If you don't have a job or your employer has closed the telecommuting door, then it may be time to look in another direction.

What are you experienced in? What can you bring to the table? Who would benefit from your

---

[18] http://bit.ly/workfromhomedf

skills? If you have worked in sales, how can you reshape yourself as an international asset?

INDEPENDENT CONSULTANT

If you have worked during your lifetime then you have experience in something. Think about what you're good at and see if you can pull together a market you can help through consultations.

There are a variety of business opportunities abroad with new business owners in every sector. These new owners need help with a variety of niches: marketing, social media, customer service practices, IT, website development, content creators, multi-media, international accounting, productivity, import/export, etc.

PROPERTY MANAGEMENT & REAL ESTATE

With more and more expats looking abroad to spend their "golden years" in a place that allows for a higher quality of life and young professionals looking for an international experience, real estate has opened up dramatically across the globe over the last few years.

With the wealthiest and largest group of people entering their retirement years, this market is expected to explode.

Don't expect to be signed as an exclusive buyer or seller agent. Look into the real estate culture and see what the norms are.

In addition to sales, property management is also a promising market. That's not to say it's easy money. Anyone who has experience maintaining property in a foreign country will tell you that it's incredibly challenging and time consuming, especially if you don't have excellent handymen and a grasp of Spanish in your arsenal. Numerous Ecuadorians and expats alike have second homes in EC. These homes need to be watched, maintained, and rented out in order to produce supplement income. With the humidity along the coastal regions of Ecuador, a house left unkept can literally rot.

TEACHING ENGLISH

You can easily earn your TESOL or TEFL certificate online or in the classroom, making you eligible to apply for teaching jobs around the world. Most employers require you to be a native English speaker, and have taken a 120 hour course in either TESOL or TEFL. Some also require a Bachelor's degree in any subject.

While taking your TEFL certification, it's possible to specialize in "young learner" or "business English" thereby adding marketability and greater appeal to land a job in your preferred target audience.

I received my TESOL certificate through International TEFL and TESOL Training. I chose the 120 unit course and completed it online with my spouse. They allowed us to turn in one homework per unit since we would be completing it together. Each assignment we turned in was reviewed by our tutor, Earl. If any changes needed to be made, Earl sent it back with remarks. I have no complaints and would recommend them: http://bit.ly/TEFLTESOL

NGOs & FOUNDATIONS

The international NGO (non-government

organization) community is enormous. Many of these organizations are in need of English speaking staff in administration, fundraising, marketing, and other job classifications. Monthly salary can range greatly.

TOURISM JOBS

Tourism is a multi-billion dollar industry. As mentioned before, the baby boomers are just beginning to enter into their retirement as the most wealthy group the world has ever seen. What do they all have in common? They all want to travel.

Group travel has always sported a healthy market and is seeing large increases in demand. This means you could hop on an established tour group as a tour director after you earn your certificate through the International Guide Academy: www.bepaidtotravel.com).

Or if you'd rather guide than direct, become a

specialized guide for a niche group: LGBT, Food, Wine, Coffee, Grandparent, or Children tours to name a few. You can earn guide certification through the National Tour Association: www.ntaonline.com. In addition to an international license, you might need to obtain your certification as a tour guide from the Ministry of Tourism in your country.

If you're a *behind the scenes* kind of person and have an artistic eye, you can secure work designing those flashy tourism brochures and website content.

WORK VISAS

Securing a work visa usually requires you to demonstrate that you are filling a position a local does not have the capabilities to fill (i.e. English language, healthcare, IT, Biotech, and International Business skills).

You will need a letter from the company that is

offering you a position specifying why they are contracting you and what importance you will bring to their company.

JOBS "OFF THE BOOKS"

Under the table jobs are more often sought out by younger folks without kids. This book does not endorse working illegally, it simply acknowledges that it occurs.

Undocumented jobs often include: restaurant work, bilingual tourism jobs (often owned by expats), flier distributer, sales, marketing, etc.

VIRTUAL OFFICE 101

Telecommuting, independent contracting, creative arts, and the freedoms provided by the worldwide web, make working from any location around the world limited only by your creativity and bandwidth.[19]

In order to work from your dream location, you will need to establish a framework. This can include but is not limited to setting up an email account, online banking, international communication solutions, business numbers in each country code necessary, mail forwarding services, securing a US address, purchasing a laptop and any devices required for connectivity to the internet.[20]

After the basics are set up, you will need to create an environment conducive to work and productivity. A space free from distractions, one that you can also walk away from when it's quitting time. Consider what you want

---

[19] Internet signal strength

[20] Cable modem, wireless router, booster, or hot spot device

your work hours to be? Are you more creative and productive in the morning or late at night?

Many 8 to 5'ers are not accustomed to the variety and freedoms allotted to those who work from home. Find out what works best for you. Experiment with your schedule until you find the best flow.

Most people feel their best with a regular sleep and rise schedule, a morning shower, eat breakfast, and get dressed for the day before they attempt to contribute to society. This is still true if you work from home. Just because you can work in your PJs doesn't necessarily mean you should.

Do not neglect your self-care each day. Take time to exercise, eat, and take breaks. It's absolutely imperative that you have a start and stop time! Telecommuting doesn't mandate that you work 24 hours a day. Just because your office and laptop are one room away, doesn't mean

you are on call 24/7. You need to set clear boundaries for yourself and those you work with. Creating a balanced schedule and sticking to it is key for a successful balance of life, family, and business.

A friend of mine, Corey Coates, owns a Podcast production company (Podfly) in addition to working for a second company as a program director. He shared,

"I start every workday early with yoga, meditation, and a light breakfast (fruit and yogurt). Then I work until lunch, when I leave for a stroll on the beach. I then return to work until 3:30pm, quitting time. I turn my phone off, close my laptop and don't think of work a minute after 3:30pm. That's the key to being as productive as I am, and not burned out."

ONLINE BANKING

Make sure your bank allows you to bill-pay, fax wire transfer information, and charges zero or minimal currency transactions fees. At the time of writing, Charles Schwab offered a High Yield

Investor Checking account with no monthly service fees or minimums, no foreign transaction fees, unlimited ATM fee rebates worldwide, mobile deposits from your smartphone, and FDIC insurance up to $250,000! See *Banking* in the *Before you Leave* section for more information.

COMMUNICATION

Business would not exist without communication. Your business may require both local and international communication options.

Let's begin with phone communication. How's your internet connection? If your service is reliable and your electricity rarely fails, then Skype and magicJack could be excellent options for an international phone solution. If you maintain international clients, you can purchase a phone number with the desired country and area code for a one time annual fee through Skype. You could

then forward all of those numbers to funnel through the same phone with the use of Google Voice. If you plan to serve the local community then you need to have an local number, most likely a cell phone for smaller one person operations.

I purchased a San Diego area code number from Skype for $60 USD for a year subscription. In addition to a US number, I was given 3 way calling, group video conferencing, and a personal voicemail. As with any internet phone service, there are glitches from time to time. I've had a few instances where my voicemail didn't pick up, and my client was unable to leave a message, but it is a rare occurrence.

With Skype, the customer can buy a subscription for just about any type of unlimited calling they desire: North America, Latin America, and world wide all starting at $2.99 per month! If you have a smart phone and a local sim card installed,[21] download the Skype app. Once you are logged in and have a strong connection to the internet through either cellular or wifi, you are able to use all of your Skype features on the go!

VIRTUAL ADMIN SUPPORT

There are a variety of administrative support options available virtually. Packages range from answering services to full-time virtual assistants (VAs). Answering services start at just 80¢ a day including a friendly operator answering the phone with your company's name. Afterwards, they either forward the call or take a message then email and/or fax the message to you. ReceptionHQ has an iPhone app that allows you to change receptionist settings and diversion numbers from anywhere in the world. They offer a free seven day trial. Try them out before you leave the country and see what you think. http://www.receptionhq.com

A virtual assistant (VA) is exactly what it sounds like, a private secretary that works from his/her home. They can answer and respond to phone calls, filter through and answer your emails, and redirect the ones that require your special attention. Common tasks also include: booking your travel, managing your personal and professional calendar, managing social media, blogging, chat room presence, and running down leads.

Tim Ferriss emphasized the usefulness of VAs in his book The 4-Hour Work Week.[22] One example of a VA company is EAHelp http://

---

bit.ly/USVAs. They provide an executive assistant starting with as little as five hours a week. I have had great luck hiring people from Elance.com and odesk.com for administrative and creative tasks.

TAXES, CORPS, & BANKING

TRICKS FOR CURRENCY CONVERSION, INSIGHTS ON TAXES AND REPORTING, & AN INTRODUCTION TO ECUADORIAN BANKING

"PAYING THE MAN"

If you register your company with your new country, make sure and learn their tax filing requirements and penalties. Hire a local CPA that has raving reviews from other business owners.

In addition to annual corporate taxes, many companies are required to report monthly! Even if you didn't make a dime, you must report what you did or did not make each month. Some countries will even fine you if you are just one day late!

INTERNATIONAL TAX

There are a variety of proposals being thrown around worldwide to create an international tax or tax on a company/ individual's worldwide income. The provocation for change is international multi-million dollar companies including Google, Starbucks, and rich individuals who have given up their US citizenship just before receiving a large sum of money from an investment or inheritance while utilizing international shields to dodge paying taxes.

The United States and other developed countries have realized that without the proper taxation of theses mega offshore companies and rich individuals, they are loosing billions of dollars.

In 2013, the US saw more than double the number of people emigrating than any other full year in the history of the United States, over 3,000 people. This shift is believed to be due to a 2010 law entitled the Foreign Account Tax Compliance Act (FATCA) which was implemented in 2014. The FATCA makes it 'legal' for the US to bully financial institutions around the world into providing account numbers of clients who hold US citizenship. This information is then sent to the good ole' IRS. Read more about FATCA in the *US Tax* section.

As of this writing, there are no taxes on worldwide income. By definition, an international tax would create double taxation. If the US is successful in creating it, they will be able to add double taxation to Washington D.C.'s taxation without representation faux pa. Keep your eye on this issue if you own an international business or have assets in a foreign bank.

MOVING MONEY

Western Union

An oldie but goodie at times. Western Union cuts out the middle man and allows you to send money to people around the world.

Wire Transfer

This is the most used and simplest way to send larger sums of money into the country. Unfortunately, times are changing. The assumption is if you are moving large sums of money out of North America, especially the US, then you must be doing something naughty with it. Since FACTA[23] passed, banks are required to ask you what you're doing with *your* money as if that's any of their business!

Paypal

Paypal can be a great way to get paid for a service or product, however, you must link it to a US bank account. So, if you're looking for a US-free financial solution, this isn't it. It also doesn't allow you to run international credit cards.

Wells Fargo

Wells Fargo has an option called "Express Send." You can wire money online from your US account to participating banks around the world for just $9. Not only is it a great rate but it's called express for a reason, it arrives in less than an hour! In order to set up *Express Send,* you must go through a two week set up process but it's worth it! They also have an account package called the PMA package[24] that allows

---

[23] http://www.irs.gov/Businesses/Corporations/Foreign-Account-Tax-Compliance-Act-FATCA

[24] http://bit.ly/fargoPMA

you two fee-free ATM withdrawals per statement period. The PMA package has a $30 monthly fee that is waived if you maintain at least $25,000 in your account.

If you send money to a bank that's not on their "special list" then they charge the industry standard $40-$50.

US TAXES

It doesn't take a tax professional to recognize that the US wants their cut of the pie. Even though you have left the States, they will still tax you. Some expats have given up their citizenship in an effort to avoid paying taxes to a country they do not live in. If your worth is greater than $622,000 and you gave up your citizenship, you may be pursued by the IRS for tax evasion. The US has even gone so far as to create an Expatriation Tax which requires the expat who has renounced their citizenship to pay taxes for 10 years after they are no longer a US citizen!

Since the US is losing people from the highest tax brackets to other countries, they have enacted a new law to deter others from emigrating. You are no longer allowed to reacquire your citizenship once you renounce it! Seems like the government holds a grudge!

FATCA- *Foreign Account Tax Compliance Act*[25]

FATCA is a government response to heavyweight tax evaders. A provision as recent as July 1, 2014 was initiated through FATCA *requiring* foreign financial institutions with US clients to provide annual reports to the IRS with the name, address, largest account balance in the year, and total debits and credits of any

---

[25] To read the argument why FATCA is bad for Amercia go to: http://bit.ly/FATCAbad

account owned by their U.S. customer. The new law is a way for the United States to monitor where you are, how much money you have, and impose a 30% withholding tax for institutions concerning U.S. securities who do not comply.

It's going to be a roller coaster ride watching this dramatic new law play out. Only time will tell how big of a mess we will end up in. Hundreds of international banks have closed the accounts of their US customers due to the outrageous demands by the US (FATCA).

You can file your US tax return through a U.S. Embassy or mail it.[26]

FOREIGN EARNED INCOME EXCLUSION

for US citizens

A potential break in the aggressive US tax requirements is the Foreign Earned Income Exclusion. In order to qualify, you must be a US citizen, your tax country must be outside of the US, be a "bona fide resident" of a non-US country, and have spent ≥330 full days there during a period of 12 consecutive months. The days are in total, they do not have to be consecutive, and are not reset on January 1st. In any 12 month span, you cannot have spent more than 34 days outside of your new country to qualify.

If you qualify, you won't have to pay any taxes on income up to $97,600. You may also qualify to deduct foreign housing costs. The annual cap for the housing exclusion is $29,280 or 30% of the maximum Foreign Earned Income Exclusion. Remodeling, decorating, and furnishing is not included.

---

[26] Go to the IRS website, U.S. Citizens and Resident Aliens Abroad section for more information.

If you qualify for the exclusion, it doesn't mean you don't have to file taxes. You are required to file if you made more than $9,750 in world-wide income. You may not pay a dime, but Uncle Sam wants to keep an eye on you.

The most popular tax forms for the expat are the standard 1040, Form 2555- Foreign Earned Income Exclusion and the Form 1116- Foreign Tax credit.

The rules for this exclusion are not simple. I would recommend using a CPA or other tax professional who specializes in expatriate taxes. This section is in no way to be used as the sole reference for tax guidance. It's simply a gringo's take on expat taxes as best I can understand. *See www.becominganexpat.com for CPAs and attorneys vouched for by expats.*

FBAR

Report of Foreign Bank & Financial Accounts [27]

Any US citizen that has over $10,000 in accumulative accounts outside of the US at anytime during the calendar year is required to report it to the US government. Even if it was for the purchase of a house, and you simply transferred the money into your international bank account where it was immediately routed out during escrow.

The filing deadline is June 30th every year. This year (2014) was the first time it was required to file online. You will need to download free Adobe Acrobat if your computer doesn't already have it.

---

[27] http://bit.ly/FBARtax

CANADIAN TAX CONSIDERATIONS[28]

If you're Canadian and planning a move to Ecuador, the government wants you to inform the Canada Revenue Agency (CRA) before you leave to work out what your residency status will be. They have a form to help you decide what status fits your situation: NR73. Numerous Canadian expats follow the stance that they can decide what their residency status is for themselves and opt not to share information.

In order to keep your GSI (Guaranteed Income Supplement) you cannot be outside of Canada for more than six months out of the year. Below is a list of other deal breakers that would result in the loss of your GSI:
• You don't file an individual Income Tax and Benefit Return by April 30, or if, by the end of June each year, they have not received the information about your net income for the previous year
• You leave Canada for more than six consecutive months
• Your net income is above the maximum annual[29] income
• You are incarcerated in a federal penitentiary for two years or longer
• You die (morbid but true)

I always advise you to consult your tax professional with important decisions such as this one. Reading through governmental jargon is seemingly impossible to decipher. So if the below bullet-points leave you scratching your head or throwing this book across the room, just leave it to the professionals.

---

[28] http://bit.ly/CanuckImmigration

[29] http://bit.ly/maxlimit

The information below covers each resident status in Canada and is quoted from a Canadian governmental website: travel.gc.ca

• **Factual residents**
  * Working temporarily outside Canada
  * Teaching or attending school in another country
  * Commuting (going back and forth daily or weekly) from Canada to your place of work in the United States, or
  * Vacationing outside Canada

• **Deemed residents**
  * A federal, provincial or territorial government employee who was a resident of Canada just before being posted abroad or who received a representation allowance for the year
  * A member of the Canadian Forces
  * A member of the Canadian Forces oversea's school staff who chooses to file a return as a resident of Canada
  * Working under a Canada International Development Agency assistance program if you were a resident of Canada at any time during the three-month period just before you began your duties abroad
  * A dependent child of one of the four persons described above and your net income for the year was not more than the basic personal amount (line 300 in the General Income Tax and Benefit Guide) or
  * A person who, under an agreement or convention (including a tax treaty) between Canada and another country, is exempt from tax in that other country on 90% or more of their income from all sources

because of their relationship to a resident (including a deemed resident) of Canada

- **Non-residents**
  - * Normally or routinely live in another country and are not considered a resident of Canada
  - * Do not have significant residential ties to Canada, and
  - * Live outside Canada throughout the tax year, or
  - * Stay in Canada for less than 183 days in the tax year

- **Deemed non-residents**
  - * If you are a factual resident or a deemed resident of Canada and are considered to be a resident of another country that has a tax treaty with Canada, you may be considered a deemed non-resident of

Canada for income tax purposes.

BRITISH PENSIONS

QROPS & QNUPS[30] are two five letter acronyms every British expat should know.

QROPS stands for Qualifying Recognized Overseas Pension Scheme, but is often called an 'offshore' pension because the providers of said pension work from financial centers around the world.

There are more than 3,000 options available across 46 countries. Some expats opt to work with a financial adviser instead of dealing directly with a QROPS provider. There are various rules and tax implications depending on the laws of the country where the program is based.

Reasons why a Brit might want to consider a QROPS include:

[30] http://bit.ly/UKexpatpension

- up to 30% lump sum availability
- inherent tax free
- portability

QNUPS stands for Qualifying Non-UK Pension Scheme. The two programs are very similar, consult your financial advisor to decide which is better for you and your family.

HOW TO LIVE FOR FREE

WORK TRADES AND HOUSE-SITTING

Living for free is not a myth or a gimmick. People are living rent and food free across the globe. This lifestyle is temporary for some and permanent for others! It can serve in financial hardship or offer an alternative lifestyle for folks who aren't attached to things, locations, and consumerism. It certainly pulls at the heartstrings of nomads.

Whatever the reason, whatever your situation, it's possible so unless you're attached to the idea of paying rent, it would be crazy not to consider!

HOUSE-HOTEL-PET-SITTING

Exactly as it sounds, if you are a house, hotel, or pet sitter, you watch and maintain the property and animals per the instructions of the owner. If you do your homework right, this type of arrangement is a win win and can be an excellent way to save money while experiencing life as a local in a new area!

There is a huge range of responsibilities from one sitting job to another. Which is why it's imperative to ask all of the right questions, gather all the information, rules, and expectations before you commit to a job. Your tasks could range from watching a house and watering plants, to a rigorous pet activity and care program that requires something of you every couple of hours. Below are some examples of websites that advertise care-taking jobs. While options in EC exists, none of the sites exist solely for Ecuador and their inventory constantly turns over.

• MindmyHouse.com
$20/year

• HouseCarers.com
$50/year
This site has room for improvement, but is an excellent choice for those seeking a house in the land down under

• CareTaker.org
$30/year
I have personally used this site, and find that it has extensive listings. The downside is it doesn't allow you to view all of the listings without subscribing.

• TrustedHouseSitters.com
$49 for 3 months
$64.00 for 6 months
$79.00 for12 months
This site offers more listings than any of the others.

Word of Mouth & Part-Time Expats

Keep your eyes and ears open for opportunities to help other expats keep their home and pets safe while they visit family back home!

You will have to put forth some effort to land a house/ pet sitting gig. After all, living for free is a pretty epic goal and competition can be fierce. The first job is often the hardest to land because you lack experience and pertinent references. The key to success is to look at each sitting opportunity as a job interview. Be professional, polite, and learn as much about the position as possible before you make any decisions.

The profile you create (with the service you subscribe to) is the equivalent of your resume. If you don't put in effort here, don't bother subscribing. Remember, these home and pet owners are looking for a stranger to welcome into their home when they aren't going to be there! Don't sound like a robot, be yourself in a respectable way and show passion. Let them get to know you through your profile.

Include examples that display how responsible you are: your hobbies, your cleanliness, pet enthusiasm, experience, your hobbies, and what you can do for them. Don't just say you like dogs, make sure and use examples demonstrating how much you care for animals (i.e. you're a volunteer for a local humane society). If you have horse, gardening, or farming experience, say so. If you haven't worked as a house/ pet sitter abroad, but have done so for family and friends include those experience and offer the references. If you have experience with www.couchsurfing.org, make sure to include that along with your user name then the homeowners can read your reviews as a guest and host on the site. When in doubt, ask for previous bosses, landlords, and even teachers to vouch for your trustworthiness and reliability.

Everyone has a special set of skills, if yours happens to be handy work, then mention it. Homeowners will feel better knowing their home will be cared for if something breaks while they are away. If you have gardening skills, marketing skills, computer skills, alternative energy skills, list them. You never know how your skills could benefit the homeowner. After all, the goal here is a mutually beneficial relationship!

Once you find a job you want to apply for, you have a chance to send a brief message along with your profile for their review. Treat this message like a cover letter. A brief introduction to what you can do for them, why their house is the job you want, and why they should hire you over other prospective sitters. Make sure to be passionate and real. Show your personality in a professional way.

Speaking of professionalism, make sure to respond quickly and professionally to each email correspondence. Write their name at the top, use full sentences, and always end your message with something to the effect of, "I appreciate your time and consideration."

Hesitation may cost you excellent housesitting opportunities. If the house is in a desirable location, the position will often be filled the same day it posts. Setting up alerts for your desired location could be the most important thing you do with your service.

Once you have captured a homeowner's interest and have answered their questions or concerns, don't neglect your own. You need to ask the right questions to insure the position is a good fit for you. Ask the owner:

- Is it ok to have guests?
- How long can the pet/ house can be left alone? (You may wish to explore a nearby town for the weekend)
- Is there a vehicle you can use?
- What is public transit like near them?
- How far away is the nearest grocery store?
- Will you have access to the internet?
- Is there warm water?
- Are there any rules you need to abide by?

MASTERING SITTING

In order to be an excellent house/pet sitter, all that's required is common sense and fullfillment of the owner's requests. Remember, you're a guest so make sure you return the home in *better* condition than you received it. Wash the linens you used, make certain the house is tidy, and if you'd like some brownie points, make some brownies! Leave something homemade in the fridge for their arrival home with a note so they know you made it especially for them.

Pay close attention to the owner's requests. If the owner asks you to leave the mail in a certain area, take care to neatly place the mail in its designated place. If they'd like you to check in via email every so often, make sure and set an alarm in your calendar to do so. If you respect their wishes and go above and beyond the minimum expectation, you will accumulate an unending list of glowing references enabling a rent-free lifestyle for as long as you'd like.

WORK EXCHANGE

A work exchange is bartering work for accommodations. It's a great opportunity to see what it's like to live and work in a new region or with a new culture without taking financial risk.

Workaway.info and Helpx.net are two great websites that allow you to search for places to work in exchange for free room and board *(On the flip side, once you decide to buy a home, you can host workers through the site to help you remodel, or advertise a new business in exchange for room and board.)*

Just like housesitting, your profile matters! Take time to construct one that really draws on your skill-set. Next, search the country where you'd like to work and the type of work that you'd like to do.

For example, I searched Ecuador and organic farm stay. This resulted is a list of organic farm owners who were looking for some extra help in exchange for room and board. The range of work possibilities is extensive. Examples of work projects include: help with new construction, marketing, refurbishing a boat, gardening, cooking, teaching English, farming, housekeeping, concierge, working with horses, etc.

The most common arrangement I've seen advertised is approximately 20 hours of work in exchange for free room and board. I'd also say that farming both organic and in-organic offer the most jobs.

Make sure and clarify your specific arrangement with the owner because every situation is unique. Some work exchanges are full-time in exchange for free room and board and an additional stipend. I've seen others that want you to pay them for some of your expenses and work full time for them.

Free room and board is great, walking away from a few months living alongside a new culture, town, way of life, with a new skill, is priceless!

The Caretakers Gazette also offers work exchanges for a small stipend and free room and board. On that particular site, I've observed work as caregiver, handy-person, and live-in hotel manager most frequently.

COUCH SURFING

Couch surfing is not just a way to describe sleeping on your cousin's couch any longer. Now, it is an entire genre of travel. People of all ages travel around the world meeting Couch Surfers from every country they've traveled.

Couch surfing is a free short-term local housing solution. The average stay is two nights. It's a great way to travel around EC searching for the region that best suits you, and gathering information and advice from locals and expats who have already made the move.

www.CouchSurfing.org is a site whose slogan is, *"Changing the world one couch at a time."* To experience this new way of travel, all you need to do is sign up and create a free profile. There, you can decide whether you'd like to host travelers, play tour guide, or simply chat over a cup of joe, and exchange stories.

You're never required to host someone, even if your profile says that you can. You can search for potential hosts, or for *surfers* looking for a place to stay in your area. If you find a "couch" you'd like to surf, simply write to them.

In your couch surfing request, tell them why you'd like to stay with them in particular. Show them that you took the time to read their profile.

Even though it's called "couch" surfing, oftentimes your host has a spare bedroom you can have all to yourself! The sleeping situation is listed in the profile of the potential host. I've couch surfed in Canada, St. Lucia, and across the United States. I have hosted surfers many times in Costa Rica and had excellent experiences making friends with travel peers around the world!

ADDITIONAL READING

- <u>Work Your Way Around the World: The Globetrotter's Bible</u> by Susan Griffith
- <u>**Remote: Office Not Required**</u> by Jason Fried & David Heinemeier Hansson

PART VI

HEALTHCARE & GOLDEN YEARS

An introduction to healthcare, supplemental insurance, retirement, & the part-time expat

HEALTHCARE

Healthcare is a big deal for most. Take a look at elections across the globe, a leading promise is always to better healthcare. Why? Because it matters. We want the assurance if we get sick and are in need of care or a life saving procedure, we will have access. In addition to a language and culture barrier, your new country will have a health system unfamiliar to you.

Healthcare is quirky and personal. Each individual's comfort level will vary. Some folks prefer to pay out of pocket and others choose to purchase a combination of public, private, and international healthcare insurances. Each plan carries a corresponding price tag and peace of mind.

PREVENTION

Below are a few illness prevention techniques:

• Take daily walks through your new natural oasis and see your mood, energy level, bone density, Vitamin

D levels, and health improve.

- Replace sugar drinks and beer with fresh coconut water (coco helado) and smoothies made from the ridiculously delicious produce. (If you're in the tropics)

VACCINATIONS

It's a good idea to go to a travel clinic or schedule an appointment with your doctor in order to discuss and receive vaccinations. Look at the **CDC** site for the country you decide to move to. Common vaccinations include:

- Hepatitis A
- Typhoid
- Hepatitis B
- Rabies *(for those who plan to work with dogs, live in remote areas, adventure travel, or caving)*
- Yellow Fever

If you have any questions or other concerns about vaccinations and other health precautions (i.e. safe food, water practices, and insect bite protection) call the Centers for Disease Control and Prevention's hotline: 1-877-FYI-TRIP (1-877-394-8747).

CARE

Sometimes, the right healthcare option for you is a matter of comfort. If you've had the same cardiologist or family practitioner for years, you have a history and trust that was built over the course of many years. Moving abroad will reset that comfort level. In order to manage this change, I highly recommend you interview doctors during your *"try before you pry"* time. Make an appointment and interview specialists that are applicable to your needs.

INTERVIEW YOUR DOCTOR:

☐Where did they complete schooling?

☐Are they board certified? *(All physicians are licensed but not all are board certified.)* If so, in what specialty?

☐How many patients have they had with my particular ailment/ condition?

☐How can you reach them outside of office hours? Cell phone number?

☐Do they respond to calls during office hours?

☐If they are out of town, who fills in for them?

☐What is their philosophy of healthcare?

☐Do they have more than one location to see patients?

☐How do they handle billing?

After you have collected all of your information with at least three physicians (preferably those you have been referred to), decide what questions and answers hold the most stout with you and score them accordingly. Don't forget to weigh in heavily with your comfort level and rapport with your future physician.

PUBLIC HEALTHCARE

You may be eligible for coverage through the government healthcare system as a permanent resident. Make sure and do your homework to decide if this is the best option for you. In some cases, enrolling in the government-based healthcare program can even make you eligible for additional retirement benefits after a period of time.

The fees are often drastically cheaper than what your home country charges. In Ecuador their healthcare system starts at just $70 a month!

Make sure you understand what is covered and what isn't. Some countries don't pay for "elective procedures" and considers a knee or hip replacement as prosthetic devices which is also not covered.

PRIVATE INSURANCE

SALUD Healthcare

Salud offers a variety of coverage from levels 1-7 ($40 - $200 cost dependent on level chosen and medical history). One is the most affordable with higher deductibles and minimal care, seven is the Cadillac of coverages with zero deductibles and access to the best clinics and hospitals.

General coverage
• 80% in outpatient procedures
• To 100% hospital inpatient
• Up to 100% in intensive care
• 60% drug coverage

Extended coverage
Expanded coverage plans give you an annual per person of $160,000 coverage.

Benefits

• Treatment of metastatic cancer, heart attacks, bypass surgery, stroke, chronic renal failure, severe burns, and major organ transplant.
• Accidental involuntary death coverage.
• Coverage abroad.
• Glasses, prostheses, orthoses and for the attentions of dentistry, psychiatry and psychology, there are agreements available.
• Physiotherapeutic procedures: 10 annual sessions by the contract person.

Prices range from $75 a month to $235 depending on your age and plan selection.

OUT OF POCKET

Healthcare abroad is often so cheap that healthy folks just opt to pay out of pocket. This is a common path for younger and healthy expats.

If you are concerned about cost, feel free to call the hospital where you would go and ask them the costs of a variety of procedures. They should have a fee schedule and will tell you the cost and the minimum you need to bring to get through the doors. Remember, in many countries, you won't be seen until you can prove payment. That fact can send those on the fence towards a government healthcare program where they know you're covered with a simple entrance of your residence card into the computer system, or private insurance where a simple confirmation phone call should do the trick.

INTERNATIONAL HEALTHCARE

There is a growing trend towards international lifestyles. If you don't plan to live in any one place full time or you travel so much you're barely at home, an international plan might be a better option for you.

Make sure the coverage that you choose has coverage inside the US if you think you may need to return within the given time period. Many insurances omit the US due to the inflated healthcare expenses.

BROKERFISH
www.brokerfish.com

This is a search option that you can use just like searching for airfare or car insurance. You enter in the ages of your family members and your desired international coverage. The most expensive factors seem to be whether or not you wish to have coverage in the US and whether or not you want to include emergency evacuation.

TRAVEL INSURANCE

If you don't plan to "stay put" for longer than 6 months at any given time then travel insurance may be your best option. An added bonus to purchasing travel insurance is besides coverage for your own flesh and bones, you can opt for insurance against lost luggage, trip cancellation, and sometimes theft! This can be a great solution for those that only want emergency coverage. It also might be an ideal option for the part-time expat, see more in the *Part Time Expat* section.

World Nomad offers amazing plans at affordable rates.

MALPRACTICE

Potential expats are often nervous about medical care that doesn't have the backing of a billion dollar medical malpractice insurance industry. After all, there is always risk involved with medical care, and if human error was made then it would be nice if your loved ones were covered.

Most countries around the world protect their physicians and are much less litigious, so if this is deal breaker make sure you understand the consequences of poor medical care in the country you are moving to.

MEDICAL TOURISM

Three per cent of the *world*'s population travels internationally for medical treatment![31] That's roughly 211,710,000 people! Patients Beyond Borders, an organization that publishes international medical travel guidebooks, reported that the medical tourism industry produces $40 billion a year in business.

---

[31] IPK International Survey

Patients requiring elective, non-elective, and dental procedures are heading abroad. Procedures are often less than half the cost in the United States. The medical tourism industry capitalizes where the US lacks. There are companies that will make all of your health and travel arrangements including taking you by hand to everywhere you need to be to accomplish your health needs.

BOOKS
Patients Without Borders: Everybody's Guide to Affordable, World-Class Healthcare[32]

---

[32] http://bit.ly/guidetohealthcare

RETIRED LIFE

REINVENTING YOU, GETTING CONNECTED, FALLING BACK IN LOVE WITH
LIFE

Live in a place where as your age increases so does your level of respect from the community.

One size does not fit all, nor does one way of retiring fit every retired individual. This transition is not to be taken lightly. Just as your transition into adolescence, adulthood, and possibly parenthood were taken seriously so too should your transition into your wisest stage.

When considering a move to another country, you are in an ideal time to sit and reevaluate the person that you are today. Your life experiences have shaped you and groomed you to be who you are, don't base your decisions on the person you were in the 60s, 70s, or 80s. Instead, decide what is important to you now, and what do you want to be important to you now? Reshape your life based on your answers. Moving abroad gives you a unique gift, a reset button to recreate yourself. Don't waste it!

PRIORITIES

Homework time! Create a priority chart, listing no fewer than 15 priorities. Next to each priority, rate its importance with a 1 - 10 ranking, one representing the highest importance, ten representing the least. Some examples of priorities include: health, relationship, learning, location, spirituality, hobbies, financial security, travel, being active, giving back to the community, and family. Make a conscious effort to demonstrate your top ten priorities through time allocation.

After you have your core ten priorities, write down what success looks like in each one. For example, for health you could write: "Walk 3 miles every morning, attend yoga 2x weekly, and journal 4x weekly." This task will provide you with a way to measure your success.

Some of you may have lived for financial achievement and success, climbing the corporate ladder to the rooftop deck. You may feel a strong challenge to reshape what success looks like to you in this new stage of your life. You might not have support staff, meetings, and other daily procedures that create a sense of importance and success.

LEARN

You can't teach an old dog a new trick... Bullshit! Learn a new skill that you've always wanted to learn. Take up fly-fishing, birding, woodworking, basket weaving, hiking, or walking. Maybe you already have a few solid hobbies, take them to the next level. Buy that table saw or tool that you need to take your woodworking to the next level, or a sewing machine, new rod, or GPS device. Read a book on how to further expand your skills, watch YouTube tutorials or best yet, find an apprenticeship.

WHAT TO DO

You finally made it to retirement. Talk about the ultimate hurry up and wait. For most people, lounging by the pool all day sipping on piña coladas will be spectacular for about a week, then what? Hobbies only get you so far. What can you do that will give your life purpose? You could seek out volunteer opportunities within the community or a field of interest. Or you could pick up a part-time job.

It has become more and more common to see "retired" folks working part-time or stepping into the entrepreneur world by starting up a business they always dreamed about. Think about projects that would be fun. Look into part-time opportunities helping local businesses in your area through consulting or independent contractor work.

Get connected through social networks near you, both expat and local. Try not to isolate yourself into the expat world, you miss out on so much of what the local heart has to offer. Invite your neighbors over for dinner once a month, start up, or attend a "Sunday Funday" with your community.

Travel and explore your new country. There are rivers, waterfalls, forest, jungles to be seen! Don't watch them on the Discovery Channel, go out and find your passion.

When in doubt, give it time. For many it can take up to three years to fully adjust to a new culture. You have a lot of new adjustments: schedule, climate, latitude, culture, language, surroundings, activities, expectations, and so on.

If you find yourself growing disgruntled, take a "time out" and evaluate why. If you are resenting something that is and always was part of your country's individuality, try to change your perception and appreciate the country for what it is. Your new mantras could very well be: "I'm no longer in a rush", "Just roll with it," and "Look around, I'm in _____, who cares if the ____ takes forever!"

HEALTHY LIVING

Most countries don't need shows like the Biggest Loser because they have high quality affordable fruit, vegetables, rice, and beans served in place of burgers and fries.

Plus, it's hard not to be at least a little bit active in the tropics or country where you've opted out of your own vehicle. There are many gorgeous trails and empty beaches to explore by foot, and if you're in the Sierra, everywhere is uphill both ways!

The biggest challenge to maintaining a healthy lifestyle abroad is monitoring your alcohol intake.

LANGUAGE BARRIER

If you move to a country that speaks a language other than your own, you are in for a bit of a challenge.

Tips for learning a new language:

For many adults, a major factor that slows down their language acquisition is fear of making mistakes. You didn't hear this from me but, a slight buzz can really lubricate the tongue and ease the perfectionism in you. It can also provide the liquid bravery needed to break through your learning plateaus. Too much alcohol and you can refer back to the previous section.

Picture a toddler learning English. They don't expect to get it right, so neither should the adult learner of a second language. They look adorable saying things wrong and you understand them. That will be you for awhile, an adorable gringo who is trying. More power to you!

LOVE LIFE

It's easy to fall into complacency, aiming at just surviving in life. Make a focused effort to rid your complacent habits and thrive, not survive! Experience each moment and appreciate what life is offering you in the now. Fall into love with life again. Just as a relationship has to be watered time and time again to keep it fresh and alive, so too does your soul and outlook on life.

If you are single abroad, there is no reason why your perfect match isn't waiting for you in the next café. I am proof of this sentiment! I met my Utah born wife in Costa Rica! You really never know where you will meet that special someone.

It's never too late for love either! My favorite Canadians met in her 50s and his 60s, married, and couldn't be more in love! They no longer have to find a partner to sail, kayak, paddle, explore the world, and love life with!

EXPEL THE MONSTERS

Most Common Fears in Your Golden Years:

• You will outlive your money
• You will lose your marbles
• You will spend your last years alone

Take action with something you are passionate about as a direct rebuttal to fear. Taking action is the opposite of being a victim.

YOUR BETTER HALF

"I won't let him retire because then he'd drive me crazy!" I can't tell you how many times I have heard this from wives and husbands quoting why they can't retire (especially when I worked at a fire station). There are other options.

- Share at least one daily enthusiasm *(bird watching, cooking, volunteering, walking, swimming, kayaking, tennis, etc)*
- Keep yourselves in good shape
- Take responsibility for your own happiness
- Let go of old arguments

Recommended Books:
- 65 things to Do When You Retire [33]
- The Retiring Mind,[34] Robert Delamontagne
- The Couples Retirement Puzzle: 10 Must-Have Conversations for Transitioning to the Second half of Life[35] Robert Taylor and Dorian Mintzer
- Aging Bravely, Shut Up and Stop Your Whining[36] by Dana Racinskas

---

[33] http://bit.ly/65tdretire

[34] http://bit.ly/retiringmind

[35] http://bit.ly/coupleconversations

[36] http://bit.ly/agingbravely

THE PART-TIME EXPAT

YOU'RE NOT QUITE READY FOR THE PLUNGE BUT WOULD LIKE TO DABBLE A FOOT IN? SPECIAL CONSIDERATIONS FOR SEASONAL EXPATS

Does selling your home, your car, all of your belongings, kissing your kids and grandkids goodbye, and shipping out forever sound too drastic for you? It may seem impossible for you to live far from your family.

There is a middle ground. If you're a parent or grandparent, there is a good chance you have lived much of your life based around other's needs and desires. Now that your kids have kids, it's easy to get swallowed up into full-time child care and more responsibilities than you had imagined for *YOUR* golden years.

The choice is yours. If you decide you are going to chase your dreams then clearly define them and see where your family fits. If living an international life full-time is too much awayness, then how about snow-birding, or halftime? Where is your balance? How long is the flight to your ideal location from your loved ones? Are there direct flights from the city where your children and grandchildren reside?

$$ LIFESTYLE

Can you afford the lifestyle you desire where you currently live on your retirement budget? If the answer is no, then ask yourself if you lived in an area overseas half of the year with more luxuries for less money would that help you fill the gap in your lifestyle goals?

Do you strive for continuity? For your six months abroad, will you want to return to the same country each time or do you think you will want the freedom to explore other affordable countries in the years to come? (if this is you, read <u>Becoming a Nomad</u>)

THE BALANCING ACT

Living in more than one location is inherently more work. There are double the utilities to turn on, off, and manage. If you rent out one or both of your homes, then you add an additional depth of complexity. Decorating, stocking, and maintaining homes in two countries can prove exhausting. In the end, most things worth doing are difficult. Living outside the box, in two boxes rather, may be the best arrangement for you and yours. Organization and planning are key components to help tame the additional responsibilities.

Good friends of mine, Lisa and Junior, have the goal of living a third of the year across three properties: their lake house in Virginia, their beach front estate in Roatan, and are currently looking for their third spot (potentially in Ecuador). They plan to rent each property while they are away, creating a passive income while living their dream. They have it figured out!

PROPERTY MANAGEMENT

For those who opt to purchase homes, rental income can be an excellent option. Vacation rentals have helped part-time expats to minimize costs and, in some cases, make handsome profits!

HOUSE-SITTERS

As homeowners, you are on the flip side of those who are living rent free! You can access the same sites mentioned before in the *Living for Free* section as a homeowner seeking a house-sitter. A house-sitter is helpful for your piece of mind, and to keep your home from attracting thieves, squatters, and other problematic situations.

If you live along the coast or in the jungle, the humidity can literally rot parts of the house if it's left unused. Rust and mold may destroy your appliances, AC units, or the woodwork in your home.

TRAVEL INSURANCE

If you spend no more than 6 months in one location at a time then purchasing travel insurance may be the best option for you. For more information see the *Healthcare* section.

THE MOVING BLUES

"Accept that in the first few months you may be brought to tears by the most innocuous of things. This doesn't mean you are going mad or failing; it's just part of the journey of adjustment to massive change. Cry when you need to then be determined to make the best of the next day."
~ Johanna: Irish Nomad in Malaysia

There are expats that have grown bitter and disgruntled. The most common cause is hyper-fixation on differences and change. They're like salmon, they flow along with all of the excitement and arrive to fertile international lands and the party is on! Shortly thereafter, they realize it is not what they thought it would be and flip a 180. They swim upstream fighting the way things are, and fighting the nature of the country that once attracted them. They're left exhausted and eventually caught, and served for dinner.

In order to have a healthy relationship, you must love

your partner for exactly the person they are today with their faults, their gifts, and everything in-between. So too, you must appreciate your new country for exactly what it is today in order to live a healthy and happy life here.

I'm hopping off of my soap box now...

In every move I've made, I experienced a roller coaster of emotions. If you plan for it, it can take the edge off *a little*. Expect to have an initial high followed by an intense low. The low is mostly due to loneliness, culture shock which will be discussed next, and inaccurate expectations.

Change causes stress no matter what kind of stress it is. Moving to an amazing country that fits you perfectly is still a stressful event. There are concerns you will have and worries of endless logistics: shipping your car, container, luggage, pets, new house, new area, language acquisition, new foods, access to utilities, etc.

A key method for quick acclimation is to go out and make friends in the community. Find out the inner workings of the community and how you can contribute! If you spend all day interacting with those you left back home on Skype or magicJack then you've only left in body and are cheating your experience.

CULTURE SHOCK

This is not a phenomena that happens to the weak. It can slug you in the face or slowly tighten around you like a boa constrictor! Merriam - Webster describes culture shock as, "A sense of confusion and uncertainty sometimes with feelings of anxiety that may affect people exposed to an alien culture or environment without adequate preparation."

There are four stages of culture shock, much like grief.

- Honeymoon phase
- Negotiation phase
- Adjustment phase
- Mastery phase

Honeymoon Phase

The honeymoon phase is the high I mentioned earlier. No wrong could be done to you or by you. You're romanticized by the differences in the culture, pace, way of life, and new exotic foods. Just like the honeymoon phase in a new relationship, you are blinded to any faults of your lover's. Not until the dust settles does their obnoxious habits start to crawl under your skin, and you see the real them.

When your electricity goes out in a storm, or your water gets shut off for a day or two, or you are overcharged for a service and you can't get anyone to help fix it, those not-so-sexy parts of Ecuador sneak up and bite you.

Negotiation Phase

This is when reality settles in. When you sit down and wonder what have you done? All of the differences initially seen as romantic are all of the sudden cause for great concern. Can you really do this? Can you adjust to so many differences?

You realize how incredibly far away you are from "home" and your family. Maybe you don't know a soul in your new country. If you aren't fluent in the local language, that carries with it an invisible wall. While you can't see the wall, you feel it in every interaction. You feel it when you have trouble ordering meat at the butcher counter, or paying your water bill, finding the sugar in the supermarket, or asking the bus driver how much the fare is. Additionally, it can be hard to adjust to the tropical climate (beach goers) and new food.

This phase is not pleasant and those who successfully navigate through it are gentle and patient with themselves. They also laugh at their mistakes, learn from others, and resolve that they are no longer in a hurry and no longer in the US. They learn and adopt realistic expectations.

Adjustment Phase

During this phase you have become accustomed to some of the new changes, like how long it takes to get your food while eating out and the long lines at the bank. You no longer fight the changes, you become accepting and build your routine around them. The changes become your new normal. Your understanding of the culture becomes more in-depth here, and you begin to cultivate connections with the community.

Mastery Phase

You feel 100% comfortable in your new culture. You accept the practices and participate in many aspects of the culture. You may not completely lose your culture of origin, but you are now an expert in the way of your new country. You can navigate through any hurdle or problem as they arise knowing the appropriate course of action. You are ready to take a new expat under your wing and pass forward the experiences and knowledge that countless expats gave to you.

PACKING TIPS

Plates and Flat China

Begin with the larger items. Smaller items can go toward the top.
Wrap each piece individually with several pieces of newsprint. Next,
wrap three to five previously wrapped plates together and stand
each bundle on its edge. Never lay plates flat. Add 3-4 inches of
crumpled paper and a cardboard divider before creating a second
level.

Glassware and Crystal

Always individually wrap each glass and never put one piece inside
another. Place on the very top level of your carton and pack rim
down. Especially fragile items should be packed in a separate carton
and then packed in a larger carton surrounded by cushioning.

Bowls

Wrap individually and then nest two to three together and wrap as
an entire package. Place on end or flat. Use crumpled paper and a
cardboard divider before adding layers.

Lamps

Remove shade, bulb and harp assembly. Double wrap the bulb and
harp assembly. Wrap the base and cushion it in a dish pack or
similar type box. For lampshades, select the carton size close to the
shade measurements. Pack only one shade per container. Don't use

crumpled newsprint inside or around the outside of the shade. Glass lampshades and chandeliers should be professionally packed in sturdy crates.

Food

Of course, never pack perishable items, aerosol kitchen products or frozen food. Box dry foods in medium-sized cartons after taping any openings or tops closed. Jars should be also taped shut and wrapped as well as cushioned. Pack cans and jars in smaller cartons.

Clothing

Clothing can be left in sturdy dressers or packed in suitcases, if desired. Other foldable clothing should be packed in medium-sized cartons. Hanging clothing should be packed in wardrobe cartons. If wardrobe cartons are not used, be sure to remove hangers and pack in lined cartons. Hats should be left in their boxes and packed in moving cartons. Small boxes loosely filled with newsprint also help protect hats.

Mirrors, Glass Table Tops, Pictures, Paintings, etc.

We recommend purchasing special boxes for all but the smallest items in this category. Mirror and picture cartons can handle most items. Only one article should be packed in each carton. You will want to consider professional crating assistance for oversized or heavy items such as table tops.

Glasses and Cups

Wrap individually. Cups with handles should be cushioned with another layer of paper. Pack with rims down. Cushion and layer with crumpled paper.

Books

Pack in smaller boxes with open edges alternating with the bindings. Hardcover books, or those with fragile covers should be wrapped for protection.

Draperies and Curtains

Wardrobe cartons are excellent for hanging curtains and drapes. You can also fold them and pack in boxes that have been lined with clean newsprint.

Bedding

Mattresses must be covered to protect them from soil and damage. Appropriate sized cartons are recommended.

Small Appliances

Clocks, radios and other small appliances should be individually wrapped and packed along with linens and towels or surrounded with crushed paper for protection.

Flowers and Plants

Artificial flower arrangements should be carefully wrapped and packed in individual cartons. If possible, secure the arrangement to the bottom of the box. Cushion and label appropriately.

Electronics and Clocks

Original manufacturers packaging with Styrofoam inserts provides the best protection for moving electronic goods. If these are not available, large or medium cartons should be used and the item well wrapped and cushioned. Larger home electronics such as consoles and large screen TVs should not be packed and will be moved as furniture. Computers and grandfather clocks require special pre-move preparation.

Washing Machines

Washing machines should have all hoses disconnected and put into containers. If you place hoses in the tub or drum, be sure to wrap the metal couplings with cloth or paper to avoid damage to the tub's surface. Unplug the electric cord and tape to the back. Secure the washer drum.

Refrigerators

Refrigerators should be emptied of all food. Shelves should be secured in place or detached and wrapped. The electric cord should be unplugged and taped to the back. If there is an icemaker, it should be disconnected from the water line and drained.

Tools

Any power tools containing gasoline or oil should be drained before moving. Gas tanks can be cleaned with brake cleaner. Long handled tools can be bundled then wrapped. Hand tools should be wrapped and packed.

* Packing Tips Provided by <u>Stephen Aron with IFE</u>[37]

---

[37] <u>http://bit.ly/IFEshipping</u>

COMING SOON

Becoming a Nomad

Becoming an Expat: Brazil

Becoming an Expat: Mexico

visit:
www.Becominganexpat.com

✦To see changes in-between editions

✦For additional resources like our upcoming podcast!

✦To read our blog

✦To discover what we come up with next!

Editing

Lisa Bailey

Formatting

Shannon Enete

Photography

Cover photo: Shannon Enete

www.ingramcontent.com/pod-product-compliance
Lightning Source LLC
Chambersburg PA
CBHW070809050426
42452CB00011B/1961